Jens Milbrandt

Moving on to Next Generation IP Networks

Jens Milbrandt

Moving on to Next Generation IP Networks

Performance Evaluation of Efficient Resource Management Concepts

VDM Verlag Dr. Müller

Imprint

Bibliographic information by the German National Library: The German National Library lists this publication at the German National Bibliography; detailed bibliographic information is available on the Internet at http://dnb.d-nb.de.

Cover image: www.purestockx.com

Publisher:
VDM Verlag Dr. Müller Aktiengesellschaft & Co. KG , Dudweiler Landstr. 125 a, 66123 Saarbrücken, Germany,
Phone +49 681 9100-698, Fax +49 681 9100-988,
Email: info@vdm-verlag.de

Zugl.: Würzburg, Julius-Maximilians-Universität, Dissertation, 2007

Produced in USA and UK by:
Lightning Source Inc., La Vergne, Tennessee, USA
Lightning Source UK Ltd., Milton Keynes, UK
BookSurge LLC, 5341 Dorchester Road, Suite 16, North Charleston, SC 29418, USA

ISBN: 978-3-8364-9937-8

Danksagung

An dieser Stelle möchte ich allen danken, die mich während meiner Zeit als Doktorand begleitet und unterstützt haben.

Mein besonderer Dank gilt meinem Doktorvater Prof. Dr.-Ing. Phuoc Tran-Gia, der an seinem Lehrstuhl ein kreatives und produktives Arbeitsumfeld im Bereich der Kommunikationstechnologien geschaffen hat. Diese stimulierende Umgebung ermöglichte mir die Teilnahme an wissenschaftlich höchst interessanten Industrieprojekten und den direkten Zugang zur internationalen Forschergemeinschaft.

Auch Herrn Prof. Dr. Udo Krieger bin ich zu großem Dank verpflichtet, da er trotz zeitlicher Engpässe innerhalb kurzer Zeit das Zweitgutachten für meine Doktorarbeit fertiggestellt hat.

Meinen Dank möchte ich auch Prof. Dr. Klaus Schilling und Prof. Dr. Dietmar Seipel aussprechen, die neben meinem Doktorvater als Prüfer für meine Disputation fungierten.

Für die ausnehmend gute Atmosphäre am Lehrstuhl für Verteilte Systeme bedanke ich mich bei meinen Kollegen Andreas Binzenhöfer, Dr. Mathias Dümmler, Barbara Emmert, Dr. Klaus Heck, Robert Henjes, Tobias Hoßfeld, Dr. Stefan Köhler, Dr. Kenji Leibnitz, Andreas Mäder, Rüdiger Martin, Dr. Michael Menth, Simon Oechsner, Dr. Vu Phan-Gia, Rastin Pries, Prof. Dr. Oliver Rose, Daniel Schlosser, Dr. Dirk Staehle, Dr. Kurt Tutschku und Dr. Norbert Vicari, deren Präsenz meinen Arbeitsplatz zu mehr als einen Ort der Arbeit machte.

Als wissenschaftlicher Mitarbeiter arbeitete ich viel mit studentischen Hilfskräften, Praktikanten, Studienarbeitern und Diplomanden (Sebastian Gehrsitz, Matthias Hartmann, Korbinian Humm, Jan Junker, Stefan Kopf, Andreas Reifert,

Christian Schneiker, Stephan Seufert, Florian Zeiger und Tobias Ziermann) zusammen und möchte mich bei dieser Gelegenheit für ihren Einsatz und ihre Beiträge, welche mir die Arbeit oftmals sehr erleichterten, recht herzlich bedanken.

Nicht zuletzt gebührt mein Dank unserer Sekretärin Frau Gisela Alt. Ihr Wirken am Lehrstuhl erleichterte nicht nur den Umgang mit den Formalien der täglichen Arbeit sondern bescherte auch viele schöne Stunden bei den von Ihr organisierten Festlichkeiten.

Mein abschließender Dank gilt meiner Familie, denn Sie hat mir nicht nur die Möglichkeit gegeben, mich entsprechend meiner Neigungen zu entwickeln. Auch den notwendigen Rückhalt und Zuspruch bei der Erreichung meiner beruflichen Ziele habe ich vor allem in meinem Familienkreis gefunden.

Acknowledgements

At this occasion I would like to express my gratitude to all who accompanied and supported me during my time as a PhD student.

Special thanks belong to my PhD advisor Prof. Dr.-Ing. Phuoc Tran-Gia who created at his department a creative and productive environment for working in the field of communication technologies. This stimulating environment made it possible for me to participate in scientifically most interesting industry projects and to access directly to the international research community.

I also owe many thanks to Prof. Dr. Udo Krieger who, despite a lack of time, provided the second assessment for my PhD thesis in a short period of time.

More thanks belong to Prof. Dr. Klaus Schilling and Prof. Dr. Dietmar Seipel who acted as examiners in my disputation beside my supervisor.

For the excellent atmosphere at the Department of Distributed Systems, I would like to say thank you to my colleagues Andreas Binzenhöfer, Dr. Mathias Dümmler, Barbara Emmert, Dr. Klaus Heck, Robert Henjes, Tobias Hoßfeld, Dr. Stefan Köhler, Dr. Kenji Leibnitz, Andreas Mäder, Rüdiger Martin, Dr. Michael Menth, Simon Oechsner, Dr. Vu Phan-Gia, Rastin Pries, Prof. Dr. Oliver Rose, Daniel Schlosser, Dr. Dirk Staehle, Dr. Kurt Tutschku und Dr. Norbert Vicari, whose presence at the department turned this place into more than just a simple place of work.

As a staff member of the department, I had frequent cooperations with student assistants, laboratory students, and master students (Sebastian Gehrsitz, Matthias Hartmann, Korbinian Humm, Jan Junker, Stefan Kopf, Andreas Reifert, Christian Schneiker, Stephan Seufert, Florian Zeiger und Tobias Ziermann). Thank you to all these people, as well. Their efforts and contributions often relieved me in busy times.

Last but not least, my thanks go to our secretary, Mrs. Gisela Alt. Her appearance at the department not only relaxed the dealing with the formalities of the daily bussiness but also brought many lovely hours at the festivities which she organized.

Finally, I would like to thank my family who gave me not only the possibility to grow according to my talents and preferences but also the necessary support and encouragement to reach my professional goals.

Contents

Contents

1 Introduction

Next generation networks (NGNs) must integrate the services of current circuit-switched telephone networks and packet-switched data networks. This convergence towards a unified communication infrastructure necessitates from the high *capital expenditures* (CAPEX) and *operational expenditures* (OPEX) due to the coexistence of separate networks for voice and data. In the end, NGNs must offer the same services as these legacy networks and, therefore, they must provide a low-cost packet-switched solution with real-time transport capabilities for telephony and multimedia applications. In addition, NGNs must be fault-tolerant to guarantee user satisfaction and to support business-critical processes also in case of network failures.

A key technology for the operation of NGNs is the *Internet Protocol* (IP) which evolved to a common and well accepted standard for networking in the Internet during the last 25 years. IP is easy to use and almost all networking devices support it. The *operation, administration and maintenance* (OA&M) of IP networks is partly automated and scalable. However, IP has no particular means of supporting real-time communications that require *quality of service* (QoS) guarantees in terms of packet loss and packet delay. Furthermore, the fault-tolerance in conventional IP networks is limited to the signaling and recalculation of routing tables which leads to unacceptably long reconvergence intervals after a failure.

There are two basically different approaches to achieve QoS in IP networks. With *capacity overprovisioning* (CO), an IP network is equipped with sufficient bandwidth such that network congestion becomes very unlikely and QoS is maintained most of the time. CO causes increased CAPEX in terms of capacity costs,

1

but low OPEX since resource management and human assisted operation costs are low. Moreover, no complex hardware or software is required with CO, billing systems can be simple, and only little coordination among network entities is necessary. For these reasons, CO is an appealing option for today's *Internet service providers* (ISPs). However, methods to determine the appropriate amount of over-provisioned bandwidth are difficult to design and have been investigated for only a short period of time by now. The second option to achieve QoS in IP networks is *admission control* (AC). AC represents a network-inherent intelligence that admits real-time traffic flows to a single link or an entire network only if enough resources are available such that the requirements on packet loss and delay can be met. Otherwise, the request of a new flow is blocked. AC causes increased OPEX because it makes the network and router operations more complex. It also needs more human interaction and control than CO and requires interoperability among the ISPs to achieve *end-to-end* (e2e) QoS. However, AC limits CAPEX to a modest amount and turns potential QoS violations due to capacity shortage into call blocking. In addition, it can prevent unexpected overload due to traffic changes caused by, e.g. new network applications, BGP route changes, or internal network failures and thus protects the admitted traffic.

1.1 Contribution

This work focuses on resource management and control mechanisms for NGNs, in particular on AC and associated bandwidth allocation methods. We begin with a short introduction to the IP and *(generalized) multi-protocol label switching* ((G)MPLS) technologies, then summarize the state of the art concerning QoS in the Internet, and raise issues on network resource management.

The first contribution consists of a new link-oriented AC method called *experience-based admission control* (EBAC) which is a hybrid approach dealing with the problems inherent to conventional AC mechanisms like *parameter-based* or *measurement-based AC* (PBAC/MBAC). PBAC provides good QoS but suffers from poor resource utilization and, vice versa, MBAC uses resources efficiently but is susceptible to QoS violations. Hence, EBAC aims at increasing the resource efficiency while maintaining the QoS which increases the revenues of ISPs and postpones their CAPEX for infrastructure upgrades.

To show the advantages of EBAC, we first review today's AC approaches and then develop the concept of EBAC. EBAC is a simple mechanism that safely overbooks the capacity of a single link to increase its resource utilization. We evaluate the performance of EBAC by its simulation under various traffic conditions. For static traffic, EBAC reaches steady state and its performance is measured by the achievable overbooking factor and the resulting packet delay. In the presence of traffic changes, the transient behavior of EBAC can be studied and its performance is measured by the link utilization and the reaction time of EBAC, i.e., the time required by EBAC to adapt the overbooking factor to current traffic conditions. We further extend the EBAC concept such that the overbooking mechanism is aware of different traffic types. This improves the EBAC performance with regard to traffic changes on the flow scale level. Despite its link-oriented design, EBAC is well applicable in a network-wide scope without the need for link-by-link application. For that purpose, it may be applied to virtual *border-to-border* (b2b) capacity tunnels within, e.g., a (G)MPLS network where *label switched paths* (LSPs) may implement the tunnels.

The second contribution concerns dynamic resource allocation in transport networks which implement a specific *network admission control* (NAC) architecture. In that architecture, traffic is carried through admission-controlled capacity tunnels established between all pairs of border routers in the network. The tunnels allocate portions of the link capacities in the network. They have either constant or variable size, i.e., capacity is assigned to the tunnels by either *static bandwidth allocation* (SBA) or *adaptive bandwidth allocation* (ABA). With SBA, the tunnels suffer from over- and under-utilization in the presence of changing traffic demands. In contrast, ABA continuously adapts the tunnel sizes to the current traffic conditions. Both methods lead to different AC systems. In general, the performance of different AC systems may be evaluated by conventional methods such as call blocking analysis which has often been applied in the context of multi-service *asynchronous transfer mode* (ATM) networks. However, to yield more meaningful results than abstract blocking probabilities, we propose a new method to compare different AC approaches by their respective bandwidth requirements. In particular, a network dimensioning approach is provided that calculates the capacity requirements of tunnel-based AC with either SBA or ABA. Afterwards, the bandwidth savings achievable with ABA are determined. They directly decrease the CAPEX of ISPs with regard to the deployed overall network capacity.

To present our new method for comparing different AC systems, we first give an overview of *network resource management* (NRM) in general. Then we present the concept of ABA for capacity tunnels and describe its requirements on the network and feasible implementations. Afterwards, the analytical performance evaluation framework to compare different AC systems by their capacity requirements is illustrated. The corresponding network dimensioning approach yields the required network capacities for tunnel-based AC with SBA and ABA. Different network characteristics influence the resulting bandwidth savings. Therefore, the impact of various traffic demand models and tunnel implementations, and the influence of resilience requirements on the bandwidth savings potential of ABA is investigated.

1.2 Outline

The remainder of this work is structured as follows:

Chapter 2 gives a short introduction to NGN key technologies such as the Internet protocol and (generalized) multi-protocol label switching, and also discusses issues on quality of service and network resource management.

Chapter 3 presents *experience-based admission control* (EBAC). It starts with an overview of AC in general and then provides details on the conceptual design of the EBAC mechanism and on its performance evaluation by simulation.

The performance of EBAC in steady state, i.e. for rather constant traffic, is investigated. The results give a proof of concept for EBAC, allow for recommendations regarding the EBAC system parameters, and show the robustness of EBAC against traffic variability. Afterwards, the performance of EBAC in the presence of traffic changes is evaluated for decreasing and increasing traffic intensity. To improve the concept, we make EBAC aware of different traffic types and extend it towards *type-specific overbooking* (TSOB). The concept extension is described in detail and the performance of conventional EBAC and EBAC with TSOB is compared. The chapter ends with a proposal for the application of EBAC in a network scope.

Chapter 4 presents *adaptive bandwidth allocation* (ABA) for admission-controlled capacity tunnels. In the beginning, various issues on network resource management are discussed and the concept of ABA for capacity tunnels, its requirements on the underlying network architecture, and two alternative implementations are presented. The subsequently developed performance evaluation framework consists of a general capacity dimensioning algorithm that is based on the inverted Kaufman-Roberts formula for the calculation of blocking probabilities, and that is customized to yield the required tunnel capacities for *static bandwidth allocation* (SBA) and ABA. Using different procedures specific to the bandwidth allocation methods, the overall required network capacity is finally calculated for SBA and ABA. The difference between these capacities represents the bandwidth savings that can be achieved with ABA. The savings potential of ABA depends on many network characteristics such as the supposed traffic demand model, the applied tunnel implementation, and the question if network resilience should be considered or not. Numerical results illustrate the impact of all these factors on the achievable bandwidth savings.

Finally, Chapter 5 summarizes this work.

1 Introduction

2 Next Generation Network (NGN) Key Technologies

This chapter gives an introduction to key technologies for next generation networks (NGNs). The Internet protocol (IP) is described in detail because it will be the base technology for NGNs. In addition, the (generalized) multi-protocol label switching ((G)MPLS) technology is considered since it allows for an easy implementation of network capacity tunnels for which we propose adaptive bandwidth allocation in Chapter 4. Finally, we discuss issues on quality of service (QoS) and network resource management (NRM) because they are mostly missing in today's Internet and are indispensable for NGNs.

2.1 Internet Protocol (IP) Technology

In the past decades, the Internet protocol (IP) architecture [1, 2] has evolved to the most important technology for worldwide communication. Therefore, IP will be fundamental for NGN solutions. The details on IP are presented after a short introduction to communication protocols and the concept of protocol layering. To complete the big picture of Internet communication, some examples of higher layer protocols are explained that enable seamless communication between end systems. Furthermore, the structure of today's Internet is illustrated, the addressing scheme of IP is explained, and the forwarding of IP datagrams based on routing tables is illustrated. These routing tables are automatically built by routing protocols that are essential elements of the IP technology.

2.1.1 Communication Protocols

Communication protocols enable the communication between remote systems. They are used to exchange messages that must be interpreted equally by all communication participants. For heterogeneous remote systems developed by different vendors, the protocol specifications must be available to the public. The protocols for Internet communication are standardized by the *Internet Engineering Task Force* (IETF) [3] whose standards are called "Request for Comments" (RFCs). These protocols are used in a stacked fashion and, in their entirety, build the Internet protocol stack.

Protocol Layering

We consider web surfing to explain the principle of the Internet protocol stack and to illustrate the use of layered protocols in a top-down fashion. When a user clicks on a hyperlink containing a uniform resource locator (URL), the web browser generates a request message to the computer hosting the URL. A web server program, running on the remote computer, processes this message and sends the content associated with the URL back to the web browser. The structure and interpretation of such messages is defined by the hypertext transfer protocol (HTTP) used for communication between web browser and web server. If a client program, e.g. a web browser, contacts a server program at a well-known location, we speak of client–server communication.

HTTP is an example for an application layer (AL) protocol located on top of the Internet protocol stack shown in Figure 2.1. When two processes on remote machines, e.g. client and server program, communicate, the exchanged messages must be addressed with local port numbers on the message sender and the message receiver side to enable correct message delivery.

For that reason, HTTP usually runs on top of the transmission control protocol (TCP) [4] which is a transport layer (TL) protocol defining the port numbering at the local machines. The TCP-related data is called a protocol header and is attached to the HTTP message which, in turn, is the protocol payload of TCP.

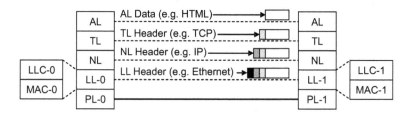

Figure 2.1: *Different layers representing the Internet protocol stack.*

The packet containing the HTTP and TCP information must be conveyed, possibly over several intermediate hops, to the destination computer. Finding a way to the destination is a matter of the Internet protocol (IP) which is a network layer (NL) protocol. IP standardizes the address space of network devices in the Internet and some other aspects. The IP header is prepended to the TCP header and the HTTP message. The resulting packet is also known as IP datagram. The consecutive application of various protocols is called protocol layering or stacking.

The logical link control (LLC) translates IP datagrams into encapsulated bit patterns, also called frames, such that the beginning and the end of a frame can be recognized in a continuous bit stream. In addition, the LLC adds a checksum to the frames to verify whether the bit patterns of the IP datagrams have been transmitted correctly. The point-to-point protocol (PPP) performs these tasks on a point-to-point link. Another widely used protocol is the high-level data link control (HDLC) protocol. The media access control (MAC) regulates the access of network devices to a physical medium if several devices share a common medium. For instance, the well-known ethernet protocol implementing the carrier sense multiple access with collision detection (CSMA/CD) [5] principle is a MAC layer protocol that controls the access to a common bus shared by several attached stations. Together, LLC and MAC constitute the link layer (LL) of the protocol stack.

The physical layer (PL) transforms bits into physical signals that are transmitted hop by hop between network devices. The protocol stack in Figure 2.1 applies to a typical Internet scenario and deviates slightly from the original open system interconnection (OSI) model defined by the International Standardization Organization (ISO). Compared to the Internet protocol stack, the ISO/OSI model is rather academic. The size of a transmitted data unit grows as headers are consecutively attached to it. When the data units is passed on from the source over several intermediate network devices to the destination, almost all information related to the AL, TL, and NL protocols remain unchanged, while the information attached by LL and PL protocols is renewed for each hop.

2.1.2 The IP Protocol

We motivate the necessity for a network layer abstraction like IP to enable transparent communication across network boundaries and, thereafter, details on the IP protocol are presented.

Inter-Networking

There are many types of physical transmission media used for data transportation. For their operation, these media require hardware-specific protocols on the physical and the link layer, i.e., various PL and LL protocols are deployed in different networks and they are not necessarily compatible. Communication based on a specific link layer is thus only possible within a single homogeneous network infrastructure. However, data exchange among multiple and physically different networks is a prerequisite for global communication. Therefore, a network layer abstraction like IP with its unifying addressing scheme is required to transport higher layer data transparently over heterogeneous networks.

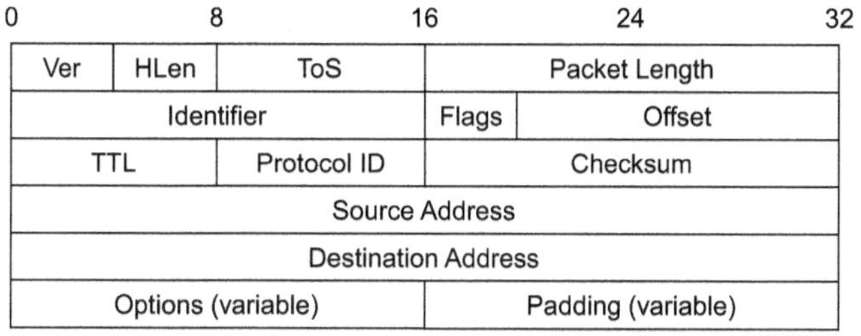

0	8	16	24	32

Ver	HLen	ToS	Packet Length	
Identifier			Flags	Offset
TTL		Protocol ID	Checksum	
Source Address				
Destination Address				
Options (variable)			Padding (variable)	

Figure 2.2: *Structure of the IPv4 header.*

The IP Header

IP datagrams traversing the Internet are equipped with an IP header whose layout is shown in Figure 2.2 [6]. The first 4 bits indicate the IP version of the datagram. The next 4 bits show the length of the IP header in multiples of 32 bit. The header length is variable due to optional fields at the end of the header. To fit the header size to a 32 bit multiple, it is padded with zeros. The 8 bits of the type of service (ToS) field can optionally be used to assign a priority class to the datagram whose entire length in bytes including the header is represented by the following 16 bits. The 16 bit identifier field is required if a packet, on its way from source to destination, is fragmented into several smaller pieces due to limited link-specific maximum transfer units (MTUs). These pieces then have the same identifier. The 3 bit flag field controls the fragmentation process. The 13 bit offset field indicates the amount of payload in units of 8 bytes that have already been sent in previous fragments. The time-to-live (TTL) is initially set to a positive integer value that is decremented by 1 for each hop. If the TTL reaches zero, the IP datagram is discarded and the sender is notified with an Internet control message protocol (ICMP) message. The protocol number identifies the type of protocol used to transmit the payload. Examples are number 6 for TCP or number 17 for UDP. The checksum protects the IP header and is used to validate its integrity. If the checksum evaluation yields an error, the datagram is discarded.

The next two 32 bit words carry the source and the destination IP address of the datagram. The options field at the end of the header can be used, for instance, to implement source routing, i.e., the field contains a list of next hops that must be visited one after another on the way to the destination.

Currently, version 4 of IP (IPv4) [1] is in use. IP version 6 (IPv6) [2] has been standardized few years ago and is expected to replace IPv4. The major change in IPv6 concerns the extension of the address space from 4 to 16 octets (bytes). As more and more network devices need to be addressable, IPv4 addresses are supposed to run short in the future. Network address translation (NAT) is a mid-term solution to mitigate this problem.

2.1.3 Higher Layer Protocols

In the Internet, worldwide connectivity is achieved through the IP network layer abstraction. We now consider transport layer (TL) and application layer (AL) protocols running on top of IP. In particular, TL and AL protocols required for real-time communication are described.

Transport Layer Protocols

Transport layer protocols organize the multiplexing of data streams from different applications into an IP packet stream. They also enable a machine to assign the received data to the corresponding processes. From an application point of view, data are transmitted between so-called sockets on the sender and the receiver side. Such a socket is identified by a source and destination IP address on the NL and by a source and destination port number on the TL. A port is a local address through which a communication process is sending or receiving messages. For some server programs, there are well-known standard port numbers, e.g. port 80 for web servers. Together with the protocol ID (cf. Figure 2.2), the NL addresses and the TL port numbers constitute an identifier for individual traffic flows. This flow descriptor can be used for prioritization or policing purposes to achieve service differentiation of different flows (cf. Section 2.3.1). To reach that goal, a descriptor is inspected to check whether a packet belongs to a specific flow. TL protocols also perform other essential but protocol-specific tasks that are described in [7] for TCP and UDP as the most prominent representatives in the Internet.

Transmission Control Protocol The transmission control protocol (TCP) [4] is a connection-oriented protocol which enables reliable transmission between two communication end systems. All data segments transmitted over TCP must be acknowledged to ensure the complete and in-order delivery of the data. The actions performed by the TCP protocol are described by state machines that work in a session context, i.e., they use information specific to individual TCP sessions, e.g. the number of the last transmitted but yet unacknowledged TCP segment. Another task of TCP is flow control based on a sliding window mechanism. Sender and receiver of a TCP flow agree on a certain receiver buffer (window) size that limits the amount of data that is sent without acknowledgements for all previous data segments. In case of network congestion, the TCP sender detects packet loss through missing acknowledgements and, as a consequence, decreases its sending window size drastically. This throttles its transmission rate and reduces the amount of unacknowledged data in the network. After such an action, the TCP sender recovers its transmission rate by slowly increasing its sending window size. As its sending rate is controlled rather by the network state than by the application, TCP is not suitable for real-time communication with stringent delay constraints.

User Datagram Protocol The user datagram protocol (UDP) [8] is very simple and does not provide any means for reliable transmission. Its header is 8 bytes long and contains the source and destination port number, two bytes indicating the length of the payload, and a checksum byte which enables UDP receivers to detect bit errors in the UDP header. No flow or congestion control is applied to UDP flows that are mostly sent by real-time applications whose traffic must not be slowed down by occasional packet losses.

Application Layer Protocols

Standardized AL protocols are required to enable the interoperability of network applications from different vendors. Usually, they use the TL capabilities of TCP or UDP. We do not explain any AL protocol in detail but merely give an overview of the most prominent representatives. The AL protocols mentioned in the following are not specific to real-time communication and, therefore, they will be used the same way in NGNs and in the traditional Internet.

General Application Layer Protocols There are a lot of widely used AL protocols like the hypertext transfer protocol (HTTP) which constitutes the base of the worldwide web (WWW), the simple mail transfer protocol (SMTP) standardizing electronic mail exchange, or the file transfer protocol (FTP) used for server-provisioned file downloads. The domain name system (DNS) maps domain names of network devices, e.g. the Google web server at "www.google.com", to their corresponding IP addresses and is thus used for most communication setups.

Application Layer Protocols for Peer-to-Peer Networks In these days, peer-to-peer (P2P) networks play a decisive role regarding the amount of traffic transported in the Internet [9]. In the recent years, a lot of different P2P network architectures have emerged. As a consequence, many proprietary protocols and those under GNU public license (GPL) have evolved that focus on different aspects of P2P networking. Some protocols, e.g. Chord, content addressable network (CAN), Pastry, and Kademlia are concerned with application-level routing and object location in potentially very large overlay networks consisting of nodes connected via the Internet. For that purpose, they construct distributed hash tables (DHTs) that serve as indices for, e.g. the search of documents in P2P systems. Other protocols like Avalanche, BitTorrent, FastTrack, or the multisource file transfer protocol (MFTP) are focused on global data storage, data sharing, and rapid content distribution within a single virtual P2P network. The above list

14

of P2P-related protocols is far from being exhaustive. A good overview on P2P systems and their applications is given in [10].

Protocols for Real-Time Communication

TCP is not suitable for QoS-stringent real-time communication and UDP provides neither reliable data transfer nor in-order data delivery. These and other functionalities are added by special protocols developed particularly for real-time communication.

Protocols for Real-Time Transport The real-time transport protocol (RTP) [11] provides an end-to-end delivery service for real-time data such as interactive audio and video. This service includes payload type identification, sequence numbering, timestamping and delivery monitoring. RTP typically runs on top of UDP to make use of its multiplexing and checksum services. RTP itself does not provide any mechanism to ensure data delivery nor any QoS guarantees but relies on lower-layer services to do so. It merely assigns source identifiers and sequence numbers for the synchronization of multimedia streams. The source identifier allows a sender to multiplex several media streams, e.g. voice and video, into a single RTP packet flow and it allows receivers to identify media streams from different senders, e.g. in case of video conferences. The sequence numbers enable the receiver to reconstruct the sender's packet sequence and, hence, addresses the deficiency of UDP to deliver packets in-order. Some additional information is carried in the RTP header that can be used to synchronize the payload of RTP packets or to identify the format of the carried media stream.

A protocol closely related to RTP is the real-time transport control protocol (RTCP) [11] that monitors the QoS of RTP packet flows and conveys session information between RTP senders and receivers. In particular, RTCP periodically exchanges messages to map the timestamps of different streams to a wallclock time such that synchronized playback of voice and video is possible. RTCP also

15

provides sender reports to identify the sender and its streams, and receiver reports to give feedback on the achieved transmission quality. Applications may use this information to adapt their media coding to good or bad channel conditions. The frequency of the reports depends on the traffic rates of the media streams and on the number of participants in a session since only a small fraction of the bandwidth should be consumed for control purposes.

Protocols for Media Streaming Mutlimedia streaming of voice or video data is unidirectional and thus non-interactive real-time communication. Since interaction is not required, a transmission delay in the order of seconds is acceptable for live transmissions such as webradio, video on demand (VoD), or IP television (IPTV). Sources of streamed data can include both live data feeds and stored clips. Usually, the playback of a media stream starts after a certain amount of data is buffered. The real-time streaming protocol (RTSP) [12] standardizes the control of streaming traffic between sender and receiver.

Protocols for Setup and Control of Real-Time Communication
A challenge for ubiquitous communication is to contact a callee if his current IP address is unknown. The session initiation protocol (SIP) [13] for creating, modifying, and terminating sessions with one or more participants, solves this problem. To reach that goal, SIP provides a registration function that allows users to register their current locations at proxy servers. These servers, also called SIP servers, help to route requests to the user's current location, to authenticate and authorize users for services, and to implement provider call-routing policies. SIP invitations are used to initiate sessions. They carry session descriptions that allow participants to agree on a set of compatible media types. Supported sessions include Internet telephone calls, multimedia distribution, and multimedia conferences. SIP provides further mechanisms for call management, e.g., participants can be invited during a session, the media encoding format can be changed, and new media streams can be added. SIP can run on top of several different TL protocols.

The H.323 protocol is standardized by the *International Telecommunication Union* (ITU) [14] and has the same objectives as SIP. The equivalent to the SIP proxy is called gatekeeper. The H.323 protocol suite is an umbrella standard that is more specific about other protocols. It mandates RTP as transport protocol for media streams and requires each terminal to support G.711 encoded speech. In addition, it describes how Internet phones have to interoperate through gateways with the public circuit-switched telephone network.

Other Protocols on Top of IP

The addressing of specific port numbers is not necessary if network devices communicate with each other independently of any application. The Internet control message protocol (ICMP) [15], for instance, is used by hosts, routers, and gateways to communicate network layer-specific information such as notifications about expired TTLs to each other. Another example for direct message transport over IP is the resource reservation protocol (RSVP) [16].

2.1.4 The Structure of the Internet

The Internet consists of many interconnected independent administrative units, so-called autonomous systems (ASes). It is organized in an pseudo-hierarchical (since not completely strict) structure with different levels called tiers as illustrated in Figure 2.3 [17].

Tier-Based Hierarchical Structure   The networks of tier-1 Internet service providers (ISPs) constitute the backbone of the Internet. They are directly connected to each other and provide worldwide service. Tier-2 ISPs only have regional or national coverage. To reach other areas in the Internet, they are connected to one or several tier-1 ISPs. Lower-tier ISPs, i.e. ISPs below tier-2, connect to the Internet via one or more tier-2 ISPs. At the bottom of the hierarchy are access ISPs which sell Internet access directly to end users and content providers.

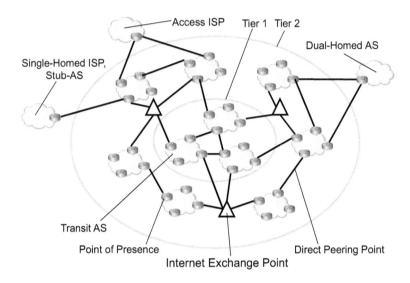

Figure 2.3: *Pseudo-hierarchical interconnection of Internet service providers.*

If access ISPs are connected to only one higher-tier ISP, they are called stub-ASes. In general, access networks implement a strictly hierarchical architecture while networks of higher-tier ISPs have a more plain structure [18]. Autonomous systems that transport traffic whose source and destination are located in other ASes are called transit networks. A unique 16 bit autonomous systems number (ASN) is assigned by the *Internet Corporation for Assigned Names and Numbers* (ICANN) [19] to every AS for inter-AS routing purposes.

A provider ISP charges a customer ISP a fee which typically depends on the bandwidth of the link connecting both ISPs. To save costs, tier-2 ISPs may also connect directly to each other and, in doing so, become peering partners. Some tier-1 ISPs also act as tier-2 or lower-tier ISP and sell Internet access directly to large companies or institutions. To remain connected to the Internet in case of

18

an uplink failure, lower-tier ISPs may be simultaneously connected to multiple higher-tier ISPs. An ISP is called single-, dual-, or multi-homed depending on its number of connected provider ISPs.

POPs and Direct Peering Points In an ISP's network, a point of presence (POP) is a group of one or more routers to which routers of other ISPs can connect, no matter whether these ISPs are on the same tier or not. End users and content providers connect to the Internet through POPs, too. For connecting to the POP of a provider ISP, a customer typically leases a high-speed link either from the provider ISP itself or from a third-party telecommunications provider. A tier-1 provider typically has many POPs scattered across different geographical locations in its network and multiple customer ISPs connect into each of these POPs. Two tier-1 ISPs may also peer with each other at multiple pairs of POPs.

Internet Exchange Points In addition to direct peering points, ISPs often interconnect at Internet exchange points (IXPs) that are owned and operated by either an ISP or a third-party telecommunications provider. An IXP is a shared interconnection infrastructure, where multiple ASes can interconnect through switches and routers at the IXP. Subject to mutual business agreements, ASes can interconnect with some or all of the other participants at the IXP. The trend for interconnecting ASes is that tier-1 ISPs connect to each other directly via direct peering points, whereas tier-2 ISPs interconnect with other tier-2 ISPs and with tier-1 ISPs at IXPs [20].

2.1.5 IP Addressing and Packet Forwarding

IP datagrams carry addresses of their source and destination for the purpose of packet delivery. We first describe the structure of IP addresses and then explain the forwarding of IP datagrams by routers which is based on the matching of destination IP address and network masks.

IP Addressing

Hosts and routers connect the links to their neighbors through physical interfaces. In general, hosts have only one interface while routers have several of them. IP addresses are assigned to interfaces rather than to machines and, therefore, hosts mostly have one IP address whereas routers have several IP addresses. These addresses are 4 binary octets, i.e. 32 bits, long and are usually written in dotted-decimal notation, e.g. 132.187.106.131. The n leftmost bits of an IP address are called the network prefix or network mask which is denoted by $a.b.c.d/n$. The rightmost part of an IP address signifies an interface within a network. The prefix length was initially restricted to values $n \in \{8, 16, 24\}$ for class A (/8), class B (/16), class C (/24), and class D (/24) network addresses. Class A addresses are specified by the network prefix 0/1, class B by 128/2, class C by 192/3, and class D by 224/4. Class D addresses are reserved for multicast purposes. Class C addresses cover only 254 interfaces within a network because interface address 0 is invalid by definition and address 255 is used for the purpose of broadcasting within a network. For comparison, class A addresses cover up to 2^{24}–2 interfaces but, due to their large address space, there are only 126 class A addresses since the network prefixes 0/8 and 127/8 are reserved. The classful partitioning of the IP address space leads to an unnecessary limitation of network prefixes and network sizes. Since 1993, classless inter-domain routing (CIDR) allows the prefix size n to have arbitrary values between 1 and 32. A further subdivision of ASes into smaller units within such authorities is called subnetting.

IP Packet Forwarding

The correct forwarding of IP datagrams is the most important task of an IP router. For that purpose, the routers maintain routing tables that specify exactly to which outgoing interface an IP packet must be forwarded. The routing table presented in Table 2.1 serves as example in the following illustrations. A routing table consists of pairs of network prefixes and corresponding outgoing interfaces. The notion of routing signifies two different tasks. The first one is the calculation of the rout-

Network Prefix	Interface
127/8	127.0.0.1
192.168.2/8	192.168.2.5
192.168.2.96/6	192.168.2.96
192.55.114/8	193.55.114.6
193.168.3/8	192.168.3.5
0/32	193.55.114.129

Table 2.1: *Example IP routing table.*

ing tables done with help of routing protocols as described in Section 2.1.6. The second task is the determination of the correct outgoing interface for an incoming IP packet according to the routing table, i.e. the routing table lookup. The latter performs a longest prefix match between the network prefixes in the routing table and the destination address of the IP packet and thus determines the outgoing interface. If the destination address of an IP packet matches multiple network prefixes, e.g. 192.168.2.96/6 and 192.168.2/8, the packet is forwarded on interface 192.168.2.96 instead of 192.168.2.5 due to the longer prefix match. IP packets with destination addresses that do not match any network-specific prefix in the routing table are routed to the default destination (0/32) and forwarded on the corresponding interface. The interface number 127.0.0.1 denotes the so-called loop-back device which returns IP packets back to the machine itself. This mechanism is used for debugging purposes.

The network prefixes a.b.0/17 and a.b.128/17 can be aggregated to a new network prefix a.b/16. This procedure is called route aggregation and helps to keep routing tables small as the routing of the entire address space can be represented in a very compact manner, i.e., the traffic to be forwarded on a certain interface can be specified by only few network prefixes. Hence, route aggregation makes IP forwarding a scalable process provided that the IP addresses in the Internet are assigned with respect to the hierarchical Internet structure depicted in Figure 2.3. For that reason, ICANN assigns IP addresses blockwise to the ISPs which, in turn, assign them to their customers. As a consequence, all traffic to the customers of an ISP can be routed using the ISP's network prefix. Exceptions can be handled by the "longest prefix match first" rule.

2.1.6 Routing Protocols

IP packets are forwarded according to routing tables that are configured inside IP routers. The setup of routing tables is mostly done automatically by various routing protocols [21] that operate in different scopes. These protocols exchange reachability and topological information to determine for each router the next hop towards any destination IP address. ISPs are generally not willing to disclose information about their networks and the applied routing to their competitors. Moreover, the entire Internet is simply too large for the global exchange of detailed routing information. Therefore, routing in the Internet is done in an hierarchical fashion that reflects the structure of the Internet (cf. Figure 2.3). Each AS represents an autonomous routing domain where the routing of AS-internal IP addresses can be done independently of other ASes. This is called intra-domain routing and performed by interior gateway routing protocols (IGPs). A gateway is a router that enables IP packets to cross an AS boundary. If an IP packet is addressed to a distant AS, it needs to cross a number of transit ASes. This is called inter-domain routing and the inter-AS path is determined by exterior gateway routing protocols (EGPs).

Intra-Domain Routing

Interior gateway protocols can be classified into distance vector protocols and link state protocols. They associate cost values with interfaces and sum up these metrics to calculate the length of a path. Interface costs may be set equally to one (hop count metric), set explicitly by network administration authorities, or derived automatically from characteristics like delay or utilization of the adjacent link. Both IGP types determine a shortest, i.e. lowest-cost, path from a source to a destination to avoid routing loops. We explain the two IGP concepts and discuss the routing information protocol (RIP) and the open shortest path first (OSPF) routing protocol as examples.

Distance Vector Protocols The distance vector protocol approach is based on the Bellman-Ford algorithm [22]. It requires each router to maintain a distance table that contains the next hop router and the path costs for each destination within the routing domain. Initially, the table holds only the router itself and its directly linked neighbors as destinations with path costs of zero or the respective interface costs. A vector containing the reachable destinations and the associated path costs is transmitted periodically to all neighboring routers. If a router A receives such a distance vector from a router B, A adds the costs of its interface towards B to the received path costs and compares them to the costs in its own distance table. If no entry for a destination exists or if the new path costs to a destination are lower than in the distance table of A, then the next hop router in this table is replaced by B and the new path costs via B are inserted. The updated distance information is then disseminated by A to all its neighbors and, when no more distance table modifications are necessary, the algorithm eventually converges. If an interface becomes inactive, its costs are set to infinity such that a new lower-cost path is found. A regular exchange of distance vectors causes the propagation of this information and initiates an update of the distance tables.

The routing information protocol (RIP) version 2 [23] exchanges RIP advertisements, i.e. distance vectors, every 30 seconds over UDP. If a router does not get an update from its neighbor once within 180 seconds, it assumes that this neighbor is no longer reachable. In RIP version 1, hop count was used as mandatory metric, i.e., the interface costs were all one. The maximum path costs were restricted to 15 and, therefore, a maximum network diameter of 15 hops was a prerequisite for the application of that protocol.

Link State Protocols Link state protocols are used by routers to broadcast the identities and metrics of their attached interfaces to all other routers in the network. Each router can thus reconstruct the complete network topology by evaluating those broadcast messages, the so-called link state advertisements (LSAs). Having a complete view on the network, each router locally computes a minimum cost path to every destination in the network by Dijkstra's shortest path algorithm [24]. The results of the path calculation are finally compiled in the routing tables.

The open shortest path first (OSPF) protocol version 2 [25] broadcasts link state advertisements either in a 30 seconds interval or if a topology change is detected. To check whether a link is operational, OSPF periodically sends so-called "Hello" messages to each directly linked neighbor. Other messages are used to exchange LSAa between neighboring routers. The information in the LSAs is stored in databases that are used for the calculation of shortest paths. The equal cost multi-path (ECMP) option of OSPF allows the use of multiple paths to a destination provided that they have the same costs. For large ASes, the OSPF protocol allows to subdivide the network into OSPF areas, where separate instances of the protocol run independently of one another. Each area has at least one area border router with similar responsibilities as an AS gateway router. The set of all area border routers constitutes an OSPF backbone area whose primary task consists of routing traffic among the other OSPF areas in the AS. This mechanism makes OSPF scalable by reducing the amount of exchanged LSAs.

The intermediate system to intermediate system protocol (IS-IS) [26] is another link state routing protocol specified by the ISO/OSI standard. After OSPF which originates from the IETF, IS-IS is the mostly utilized IGP in the Internet.

Inter-Domain Routing

Gateway routers are used to interconnect neighboring ASes and they are in charge of exchanging traffic destined for different ASes then their own. Vice versa, each gateway router must be reachable from the Internet which requires its network prefix to be present in the routing tables of other gateways. Currently, there are over 10000 ASes in the Internet and, therefore, the routing tables for inter-domain destinations can become very large. To overcome this issue, i.e. to keep the number of network prefixes low, route aggregation is absolutely necessary for inter-domain routing. The shortest path principle known from intra-domain routing is not feasible for inter-domain routing purposes because the various intra-domain metrics used in the different transit ASes are not comparable. Inter-domain paths are thus primarily chosen with respect to routing policies. A typical example rule for such policies could be that traffic is only forwarded to trusted ISPs that provide enough capacity.

The de facto standard for inter-domain routing is the border gateway protocol (BGP) version 4 [27]. Every AS contains a dedicated router called "BGP speaker" that exchanges information about reachable networks with the BGP speakers of neighboring ASes over reliable TCP connections. This information is stored in BGP routing tables that coexist with IGP routing tables in the gateway routers. If an AS has several BGP speakers, special care must be taken to maintain consistency. To support policy-based routing decisions, gateway routers announce for each reachable network prefix a list of attributes, e.g. the gateway router addresses and their corresponding AS numbers on the known inter-domain path. Therefore, BGP is called a path vector protocol which works similarly to a distance vector protocol. However, BGP does not send the routing information periodically but propagates only updates like route changes or route withdrawals if necessary. If a BGP route fails, it may take tens of minutes until the BGP protocol converges and a consistent view in the BGP routing tables of affected Internet gateways is reached.

Inter-domain routing imposes two challenges on the BGP protocol. Firstly, BGP speakers of neighboring ASes must exchange reachability information. Secondly, this information must be distributed among all intra-domain routers within an AS such that a shortest path to the closest gateway router (there may be more than one) is present in the IGP routing tables. The first task is performed by the exterior border gateway protocol (E-BGP). The second task is supported by the interior border gateway protocol (I-BGP) which distributes the reachability information from the BGP speakers to the AS-internal routers.

2.2 Multi-Protocol Label Switching (MPLS)

Multi-protocol label switching (MPLS) is a mechanism located between the link layer and the network layer that provides several means for traffic engineering (TE). We first describe conventional MPLS and then discuss its recent extension towards generalized MPLS (GMPLS) for heterogeneous network environments. In Section 4.1.3, we address further issues on resource management with MPLS and GMPLS.

2.2.1 Conventional MPLS

Multi-protocol label switching is a connection-oriented packet switching mechanism that uses IP routing protocols [25, 26] and other protocols [28–30] to establish bandwidth-assigned label switched paths (LSPs) in a network. It is called "multi-protocol" because its architecture [31] allows multiple network layer protocols like IP to be carried on top of it. The principle of MPLS is "route at the edge, switch in the core". As illustrated in Figure 2.4, an IP packet entering a MPLS network is routed at the network edge by an ingress label edge router (LER) which equips it with a 4 byte MPLS label – a so-called shim header – and forwards it to a MPLS core node called label switching router (LSR). The LSR forwards the packet by fast packet switching according to its incoming interface and its attached label. An incoming label map (ILM) stores this information together with a corresponding outgoing label and interface. The label switching process requires entries for every LSP in a management information base (MIB) of the LSRs. An egress LER finally removes the MPLS label from the IP packet. In practice, modern Internet routers are capable to process both IP and MPLS packets.

There are two major alternative protocols for the establishment of LSPs in a MPLS network. RSVP with tunneling extensions (RSVP-TE) [29] modifies the conventional RSVP [16, 32] known from the integrated services (IntServ) net-

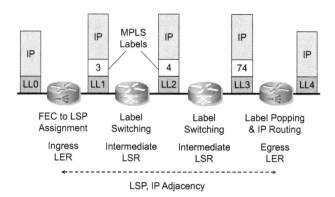

Figure 2.4: *LSP providing a new IP forwarding adjacency.*

work architecture [33] such that MPLS labels can be distributed. The constraint-based label distribution protocol (CR-LDP) [30] extends the original label distribution protocol (LDP) [28] to constrained-based routing. CR-LDP has been designed particularly for MPLS but the IETF now seems to favor RSVP-TE. Established LSPs can be associated with bandwidth reservations by using , e.g., the primitives of RSVP. They can thus be considered as virtual links taking their capacities from the physical links connecting the MPLS routers and representing new IP forwarding adjacencies. In Chapter 4, we investigate adaptive capacity tunnels that may be implemented by LSPs. Both protocols, RSVP-TE and CR-LDP, provide means for the reservation of resources whereas the more general LDP is not able to make reservations.

The label distribution and switching paradigm enables explicit route pinning which allows for a better traffic control than shortest-path routing. This is especially useful for traffic engineering (TE) [34–36]. The connection-oriented MPLS technology is often viewed as a modified version of asynchronous transfer mode (ATM) with variable cell size. However, the profound difference between the both is that ATM enables a two-fold aggregation with its virtual connection and virtual path concept while MPLS allows for many-fold aggregation by the stacking of multiple labels, i.e., a LSP may be transported over other LSPs. This feature helps to build scalable network structures, so-called LSP hierarchies [37].

2.2.2 Generalized MPLS (GMPLS)

Generalized multi-protocol label switching (GMPLS) is the logical extension of MPLS to the optical networking domain. For that purpose, GMPLS provides a multi-layer switching hierarchy which supports packet switching (PSC), time division multiplex (TDM), lambda switching (LSC), and spatial switching (FSC) as illustrated in Figure 2.5. Hence, GMPLS can be considered as a multi-purpose control plane paradigm for technology-spanning management of heterogenous network resources. An IETF working group has specified the GMPLS architecture [38] and further RFCs [39] for the standardization of GMPLS. Some of these RFCs are focused on necessary enhancements to existing MPLS signaling and IP routing protocols. Others are dedicated to GMPLS network recovery which is an important issue for QoS-enabled transport networks. Besides the standards, different aspects of the GMPLS technology and its application for TE are summarized in [40–42].

GMPLS adopts all means for TE from MPLS. With regard to the heterogeneity of LSPs in GMPLS, the construction of LSP hierarchies [43] is supported by LSP nesting (cf. Figure 2.5), i.e., lower-order LSPs are aggregated into higher-order LSP like multiple wavelengths are bundled on a single fiber. GMPLS also uses link bundling as a new means for TE to reduce routing information, i.e., multiple parallel logical links between adjacent nodes can be bundled and advertised as a single link to the routing protocol. LSP nesting and link bundling are intended to improve the scalability of GMPLS networks. Another important characteristic of GMPLS is the strict separation of data forwarding and network control which are managed on different planes. The data plane is focused on data transportation and used only for fast connection-switching between different types of LSPs. In contrast, the control plane is used for all signaling tasks performing resource

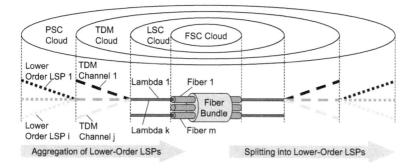

Figure 2.5: *Multi-layer switching hierarchy in the GMPLS architecture.*

discovery, dissemination of topology state information, channel management, or fault isolation. The link management protocol (LMP) [44] running between adjacent GMPLS network nodes has been specified for this purpose. LMP makes the underlying links more manageable and automates label association through all switching layers.

2.3 Issues on Quality of Service and Resource Management

Due to economical reasons, a convergence of conventional communication systems such as telephony networks, and IP networks like the Internet into a NGN architecture is desirable. Traditional telecommunication networks have three revenue generating properties:

- They offer quality of service (QoS) in terms of limited packet loss, delay, and jitter which denotes the delay variation among the packets of a flow. The associated premium services support interactive real-time communication such as telephony or more demanding multimedia applications like video conferencing or mission-critical telematic applications.

- They are highly efficient, i.e., they allow for high resource utilization due to the simple structure and easy management of homogeneous network resources like the 64 Kbit/s integrated services digital network (ISDN) channels in the traditional public switched telephone networks (PSTNs).

- They provide high reliability which is required for carrier grade networks and business-critical applications such as virtual private networks (VPNs). Business customers want a 99.999% service availability and they are not willing to bear the consequences of network outages.

In IP networks, routers switch and forward packets received from input interfaces to output interfaces. In between, the packets may be queued before they can be switched or sent through the output interface. Packet delay may occur in the routers if the fill levels of the queues increase due to congestion in the switching fabric or on the outgoing interface. Since the queues have limited size, they can overflow in case of traffic overload such that packets are discarded, i.e., packet loss occurs at the IP level. Packet loss and delay can be avoided if routers and links provide sufficient resources to carry the traffic or, vice versa, if the traffic load is kept low enough for the available tranmission capacity.

The enforcement of QoS constraints requires the allocation of network resources dedicated to high-quality communication services [45]. In general, requested network resources are expressed by bandwidth demands that bind a fraction of the network capacity if granted. To guarantee a high resource efficiency, the network resources have to be managed appropriately which is a rather complex task with regard to the heterogeneity of resources in currently deployed networks.

The availability of IP networks is endangered by network outages. Routers can fail due to software bugs, bad configurations, or hardware crashes. Links may fail due to physical damage. As a consequence, some network regions may become unreachable. If a route in a network fails, the automatic reconstruction of routing tables by the routing protocols provides an alternative path if such a path exists in the current topology. So far, the process of finding a deviation route takes in the order of minutes if the timers of the routing protocols are set to default values. Currently, the IETF aims at decreasing the reconvergence time of IP routing protocols and, therefore, develops the IP fast reroute (IP-FRR) framework [46]. Alternatively, MPLS fast reroute (MPLS-FRR) [47] may be used to deviate traffic at the routers closest to an outage location to achieve a fast failure reaction.

Future networks will be packet-switched to support the connectionless IP technology but they also have to provide QoS and high reliability to satisfy customers and, simultaneously, efficient resource utilization to maximize providers' revenues. Service differentiation, capacity overprovisioning, and admission control are approaches to introduce QoS in packet-switched networks. Network resource management helps to achieve efficiency and reliability in NGNs.

2.3.1 Service Differentiation

Internet traffic is partitioned and classified to enable service differentiation in IP networks. High-priority packets are served preferentially to reduce their loss and delay in overload situations. They may, for example, overtake low-priority packets in the queues of a router. In addition, low-priority packets may be discarded with a larger probability to leave the buffer space for high-priority packets. However, such mechanisms only lessen the effects of congestion on high-priority traffic. They cannot prevent that massive overload leads to QoS degradation. In the following, the differentiated services framework is introduced which implements preferential treatment of IP taffic on the packet level. Buffer management and packet scheduling disciplines in routers can adjust the packet loss and delay among different traffic classes.

Differentiated Services

The differentiated services (DiffServ) framework [48] introduces different traffic classes. Corresponding per-hop behaviors (PHBs) define how packets of these classes are forwarded by routers. Therefore, the terms traffic class and PHB are equivalent in the DiffServ context. The differentiated services code point (DSCP) indicates the PHB of an IP packet in the ToS field of its IP header and packets are labeled with DSCPs either by hosts or by access routers. Traffic conditioners at the network edge limit the rate of the classified traffic entering the network. The PHB-specific rates are monitored and, depending on the policy, different actions may be performed:

- Incoming packets are marked as in- or out-of-profile according to the conditions specified in a service level agreement (SLA). This is done on an aggregate basis, i.e., packets are treated unaware of the flows they belong to. One possibility is to discard packets that are marked out-of-profile.

- A second policy is downgrading the traffic to the best effort class.

- A third option is to carry the excess traffic according to its PHB and to discard the marked packets only if overload occurs. This is called policing.

- Finally, traffic conditioners may act as spacers, i.e., they may delay packets until they are in-profile according to the SLA conditions. They discard packets only if the spacer buffers overflow.

The DiffServ concept scales well since only a few PHBs have to be supported by the routers. The original IP approach is only marginally modified because the DSCP is recorded in the already existing ToS field. However, service differentiation on the packet level likewise impairs the QoS of all flows belonging to a PHB [49]. For applications with stringent QoS requirements, it is preferable to block some flows entirely in overload situations and to provide high QoS for some others. This mechanism is called admission control (AC) and will be the focus of Chapter 3.

Buffer Management and Packet Scheduling

The implementation of PHBs simultaneously accounts for buffer management and packet scheduling algorithms.

Buffer management mechanisms decide whether or not routers should buffer received packets in their queues if the forwarding is interrupted due to congestion. In case of buffer overflow, packets are usually discarded. This simple buffer management policy is called drop tail. Random early detection (RED) gateways [50] discard packets based on PHB-specific probabilities that depend on the buffer occupation.

Packet scheduling is an online algorithm that determines the order in which buffered packets are leaving the queue. The normal proceeding is first-in-first-out (FIFO) scheduling which does not distinguish between different PHBs. Static priority (SP) scheduling strictly prefers packets of higher priority classes to be forwarded, and it delays packets of lower priority classes until no more high-priority packets are buffered. Other scheduling mechanisms like generalized processor sharing (GPS) [51] or weighted fair queuing (WFQ) [52] serve packets of different traffic classes according to predefined fractions of the next-hop processor capacity that may correspond to a link bandwidth. Weighted round robin (WRR) [53] can be considered as an easy to implement approximation of WFQ. Earliest deadline first (EDF) [54] requires deadlines indicated in the packet headers. EDF serves the packet with the earliest deadline first which requires searching or sorting in real-time.

2.3.2 Overprovisioning

A resource-extensive solution to provide QoS in IP networks is capacity overprovisioning (CO) [55], i.e., the network is equipped with sufficient bandwidth such that congestion becomes unlikely. Since CO does not limit the traffic to avoid overload, all flows are admitted. CO can be combined with different traffic classes by implementing priority scheduling mechanisms. Low priority traffic can use the bandwidth provisioned for high priority traffic under non-overlad situations without additional mechanisms. Bandwidth provisioning procedures are fundamentally different from access to core networks due to the different degrees of traffic aggregation. Access networks have a limited aggregation level and their physically constrained ingress lines allow for an estimation of the peak rate traffic on the network links. Large core networks have a high level of aggregation and the traffic peak rates on the links depend significantly on the stochastic arguments of multiplexing [55]. Bandwidth provisioning can be based on traffic forecasting [56] that initially requires link measurements to determine the current traffic intensity. In addition, traffic forecasts must account for sudden load changes which may be due to internal network outages or external BGP route changes [57]. Such unplanned events make traffic forecasting and CO a difficult task. Since no modifications to the dominating IP technology are required, CO is quite appealing to today's ISPs. Practical experience shows that CO is already applied since the utilization of core networks is very low nowadays [58]. However, there is little known evidence of how much extra bandwidth is required to have a sufficiently low overload probability. The resource efficiency of CO has only been investigated for a short time [59,60] and is a critical question for economical considerations.

2.3.3 Admission Control

Service differentiation and CO avoid congestion by preferring high-priority traffic in the routers and by providing sufficient network capacity. However, they do not limit the amount of traffic in a network, which is the actual cause for congestion and subsequent packet loss and delay. The limitation of high-priority traffic is performed by admission control (AC), i.e., QoS-demanding flows must be explicitly admitted for transmission at a declared rate. Hence, AC guarantees the QoS of admitted flows at the expense of flow blocking. The transmission rates of admitted flows are controlled by traffic conditioners such as spacers or policers.

Figure 2.6 gives a schematic overview of the relation between AC and the resource reservation process for QoS-stringent flows in IP networks. An imple-

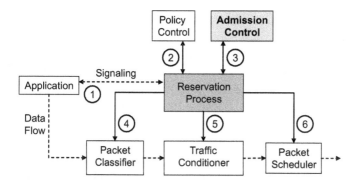

Figure 2.6: *Admission control as part of the resource reservation process.*

mentation following this procedure is given by the integrated services (IntServ) network architecture. Initially, a resource reservation request is signaled by an application to the reservation process in a router by the means of a resource reservation protocol like RSVP. The request contains information about QoS requirements (e.g. delay constraints or traffic class), traffic descriptors (e.g. mean and peak data rate) [61], and flow specifiers that identify the packets of a flow. The reservation process first authenticates the flow using a policy control module. Based on the information in the flow request, the AC entity then decides whether the new flow can be supported without violating the QoS of already admitted flows. If the new flow is accepted, the flow specifiers are propagated to the packet classifier in the router. The traffic conditioner receives the traffic descriptors and the packet scheduler is notified about the QoS requirements of the newly admitted flow. If the reservation is established, incoming data packets are associated with their corresponding reservation by the packet classifier. The traffic conditioner enforces that a data flow behaves according to its traffic descriptors and it takes appropriate actions to avoid congestion. Finally, the packet scheduler gives preferential treatment to packets with established reservations.

Admission control can be implemented in various forms. IntServ, for instance, uses RSVP to signal resource reservations along a path on a hop-by-hop basis. In this architecture, the network nodes treat flows individually with regard to their classification, policing, and scheduling, which leads to heavy overhead and scalability problems. DiffServ can also be enhanced by AC, e.g., if AC is performed only at the network border routers where traffic conditioners mark the packets with their corresponding DSCPs [62]. Core routers in a DiffServ network can then keep their simple PHB-dependent operations and remain unaware of individual flows. A drawback of DiffServ-like AC is that QoS can only be guaranteed if the resource utilization by high quality traffic is sufficiently low [63]. In Chapter 3, we introduce a new AC approach that simultaneously aims at increasing the resource utilization and maintaining QoS. A key function in all implementations of AC is resource reservation and, therefore, AC is part of the resource management in a network.

2.3.4 Network Resource Management

In circuit-switched networks like PSTNs, connections are coupled with exclusively dedicated physical resources. Therefore, only call blocking but no network congestion can occur. In connection-oriented but packet-switched network architectures like MPLS, resources are explicitly reserved by setting up paths, e.g. LSPs, with associated bandwidths. The IP technology is connection-less which actually makes its management simple. However, its connection-less paradigm complicates the establishment of resource reservations in IP networks because packet streams must be identified and related to their reserved resources.

Network resource management (NRM) in IP networks is a difficult task. Therefore, it is divided in and performed on multiple layers known as data plane, control plane, and management plane [64]. Each of these planes has its own functions and tasks to do. In the early years of IP networks, NRM was not a big issue since the offered services were simple and the corresponding amount of data was small. With increasing numbers of QoS-critical services (e.g. voice over IP

(VoIP), video on demand (VoD), IP television (IPTV)) and increasing volumes of corresponding traffic, ISPs nowadays face a great challenge. The IP technology itself does not provide sufficient means for appropriate NRM. Therefore, different technologies like DiffServ and MPLS are combined with IP to reach this goal. More details on NRM issues in IP networks are discussed in Section 4.1.

2.3.5 Prototype Implementations of NGN Architectures

The need for NGNs has provoked several pilot projects for the engineering and testing of potential NGN architectures. All of them intend to enhance today's Internet infrastructure by QoS mechanisms.

The Internet2 initiative [65] is a research consortium supported by over 200 universities in the United States that work in partnership with industry and government to develop and deploy advanced network applications and technologies for accelerating the creation of tomorrow's Internet. The European Union supports information society technologies (IST) and offers funding for projects in the so-called framework programs (FWPs). The TEQUILA project [66] is part of the 5th FWP and it concentrates on service definitions and traffic engineering tools to obtain end-to-end QoS guarantees. The AQUILA project [67] is also funded within the 5th FWP. It proposes an enhanced architecture for QoS in the Internet and, to reach that goal, it exploits existing approaches like DiffServ, IntServ, and MPLS. The PlanetLab project [68] is an open platform for the investigation and development of planetary-scale network services. The PlanetLab consists of a collection of machines distributed all over the world, provides a common software package for networking, and serves as an overlay network testbed. It also serves as a prototype for the GENI project [69] which is an experimental facility organized by the National Science Foundation (NSF) in collaboration with the research community. Its goal is the invention and demonstration of a global communication network which offers services that are qualitatively better than those in today's Internet. The EIBONE project [70] focuses on the investigation and development of robust and reliable communication networks that should satisfy the bandwith and service requirements of the 21st century. The main emphasis is on broad-band backbone networks. EIBONE consists of 18 sub-projects led by different institutions and it is supported by the Bundesministerium für Bildung und Forschung (BMBF) of the Federal Republic of Germany.

The resource management concepts presented in this work have been developed in the context of the KING project [71], where KING means "key components for the Internet of the next generation". KING started in October 2001 and ended in September 2004. It was funded by the BMBF and the Siemens AG which organized the project together with seven participating German research institutes. KING is the first NGN research project that combines QoS aspects, network efficiency, and reliability issues, and suggests a comprehensive concept for resilient QoS networks. Its goal is the development of efficient solutions for carrier-grade IP networks to satisfy high QoS and resilience requirements by means of a common approach which, at the same time, should provide low operational overheads. The network architecture developed in KING basically operates in a DiffServ-like manner. To keep the core network simple and scalable, traffic conditioners control the profiles of admitted flows only at the network edge and mark IP packets with corresponding DSCPs. In addition, a tunnel-based AC limits the traffic to such a level that rerouting in protected failure scenarios does not lead to congestion in the network.

In the following, two concepts are presented that may be used to improve the efficiency of managed resources in NGNs. The first mechanism improves resource utilization by intelligent AC in general (cf. Chapter 3) whereas the second approach enhances the previously mentioned tunnel-based AC approach in particular (cf. Chapter 4).

3 Experience-Based Admission Control (EBAC)

In this chapter, we give an overview of existing admission control (AC) concepts and propose experience-based admission control (EBAC) as a new approache to efficiently limit the traffic in packet-oriented networks. EBAC is a hybrid approach combining elements from two fundamentally different AC schemes known as parameter-based AC (PBAC) and measurement-based AC (MBAC). In the recent years, many different AC derivatives evolved that follow either the PBAC or the MBAC paradigm. Both have their individual strengths and weaknesses. EBAC takes advantage of the strengths of both paradigms and combines them in a novel AC framework that is simultaneously robust, scalable, and resource-efficient. At first, we present the basic components of this framework and describe thereafter how EBAC works on a single network link. The EBAC system has several adjustable parameters. We vary these parameters in our first investigations concerning the steady-state behavior of EBAC on a single link that carries traffic with constant properties. The results prove the correctness of the EBAC concept and furthermore show its resource-efficiency and robustness. We then analyse the transient behavior of the EBAC mechanism through simulation of strong traffic changes which are characterized by either a decrease or increase of the traffic intensity. Our results show that the transient behavior of EBAC partly depends on its adjustable experience memory and that it copes well with even strongly changing traffic characteristics. Conventional EBAC considers the traffic on a link as a whole aggregate. We therefore propose an EBAC extension that makes our AC approach aware of different traffic types. We give a proof of concept for this extension and compare its performance to that of conventional EBAC. We show that type-specific EBAC leads to better resource utilization under normal conditions and to faster response times for changing traffic mixes. Finally, we comment on the application of EBAC in a network context.

3.1 Overview of Admission Control (AC)

This section considers admission control (AC) in general, classifies existing AC methods, and introduces capacity overprovisioning as an alternative to AC.

3.1.1 General Issues on AC

AC can be subdivided into different categories which differ in their quality of service (QoS) characteristics, scope, and operation. However, they all have common objectives and the same area of application. We first comment on these common issues and then distinguish the scope of link AC (LAC) from network AC (NAC). Finally, we introduce the notion of effective bandwidth which plays an important role for classical AC.

Objective of AC

The major task of AC is to restrict the traffic transported via limited transmission resources like, e.g., a link bandwidth, a tunnel capacity, or an entire transport network. Hence, an AC mechanism makes admission decisions for new flow request arrivals, i.e., it has to admit or to reject them. If the mechanism performs well, it reaches its primary objective which is the prevention of overload on the controlled medium. If the mechanism fails, congestion occurs on the medium which leads to delayed or even dropped traffic.

Application Areas for AC

Admission control has many areas of application, especially in the field of communication networks where AC is used to manage a limited amount of available transmission resources. Different kinds of networks use AC. It is inherent in, e.g., the plain old telephone (POT) system where phone calls are blocked as soon as no more connections can be established due to lack of capacity. And it also exists in various forms in modern wireless networks [72] such as wireless local area networks (WLANs) [73] and mobile cellular networks based on code division multiple access (CDMA) technology [74].

AC mechanisms become more and more important as explained by the following example. Today's wired data and telephony networks evolve to unified and Internet protocol (IP)-based multi-service communication networks – a development that is driven by economic reasons and commonly known as IP convergence [75]. In the past, all traffic transported in IP networks was delivered according to the best effort (BE) principle. Since early network services (e.g. electronic mail (EMAIL), file transfer protocol (FTP), etc.) were simple, had almost no QoS requirements, and produced only little traffic volume, the BE delivery was acceptable. However, as new challenging network services (e.g. voice over IP (VoIP), multimedia streaming, etc.) arised and the fixed telephony and data networks are merging, there is a demand for strict QoS guarantees to satisfy the needs of customers.

Of course, different network services have different QoS requirements and, therefore, not all of them are subject to AC. In IP networks, one should basically distinguish between service differentiation and traffic classification which are orthogonal concepts. Service classes are characterized by their prioritization treatments in the packet forwarding process and their QoS requirements in terms of packet delay, packet loss, and jitter. Traffic classes are defined by their traffic characteristics which are either constant or variable. In the first case, the peak rate (e.g. in Kbit/s) of a traffic flow is sufficient to describe its character. For an elastic traffic flow, more information about its mean rate and its maximum burst size is needed to characterize its variability. AC is usually applied to a traffic flow according to its service class [76] and not of its traffic class. Hence, a flow that belongs to a high quality service should always be subject to AC to guarantee that the QoS requirements of this flow are met.

Scopes of AC

In communication networks, the scope of AC methods is focused on either a single link or an entire network. We therefore distinguish link AC (LAC, cf. Section 3.1.2) from network AC (NAC, cf. Section 3.1.3). LAC gives answer to the question: how much traffic can be supported on a single link without violating the QoS requirements of admitted flows? NAC needs to simultaneously protect a number of links with a single admission decision and thus limits the number of flows such that their QoS requirements can still be supported by a network. This makes NAC to a distributed problem where the paths of flows must be taken into account.

Effective Bandwidth

The notion of equivalent or effective bandwidth was first introduced in the context of service-integrated asynchronous transfer mode (ATM) networks [77, 78] where it is used for implementing connection admission control (CAC) – an implementation of LAC. Given an elastic flow specified by its traffic description through, e.g., peak rate, mean rate, and maximum burst size, a bandwidth value equivalent to these token bucket parameters is calculated as the effective bandwidth of the flow. CAC then implements a simple comparison of the effective bandwidth of the flow requesting admission and the bandwidth available on the link. For variable traffic flows, the effective bandwidth depends on the considered link capacity as it takes statistical multiplexing gain into account. It must be large enough to assure that the QoS requirements of all flows are met in the interaction with other admitted flows.

A good overview of effective bandwidth methods can be found in [79]. We describe some simple examples for bandwidth estimation. They assume certain traffic models and can be considered as different implementations of the effective bandwidth concept.

- With *peak rate allocation*, each flow declares its maximum rate. AC then guarantees that the sum of all peak rates does not exceed the link bandwidth. To reach that goal, the AC entity records the traffic descriptors of individual flows to increase or decrease the reserved link bandwidth when flows are admitted or terminated. The accountancy of flow-related information is also known as reservation state management. The peak rate allocation scheme requires only a small buffer to prevent packet loss and leads to little delay although delay is not explicitly taken into account.

- The $M/M/1$ queuing model [80] seems appropriate to determine the effective bandwidth of traffic flows that have irregular packet inter-arrival and service times, i.e. variable packet sizes. Several traffic descriptions for traffic with Poisson or better queuing properties are given in [81] such that corresponding policers can be constructed.

- The $N \cdot D/D/1$ queuing model assumes that homogeneous flows with a deterministic packet inter-arrival and service time, i.e. constant packet size, are multiplexed onto a single link. This model is suitable for constant bitrate real-time traffic flows. A simple queuing formula enables the computation of packet delay percentiles. An application of the formula can be found in Section 3.2.2.

- Many other methods, e.g. rate envelope multiplexing (REM) and rate sharing (RS), are discussed in [82], which is a good summary of research efforts regarding effective bandwidth in the context of ATM in the 1990s.

The applicability of these effective bandwidth methods depends on the required QoS. Hence, different approaches may be used to implement different traffic classes since, e.g., interactive real-time traffic requires more strict delay bounds than non-interactive streaming traffic.

3.1.2 Link Admission Control (LAC)

Link admission control (LAC) methods protect a single link against traffic overload. They can be further subdivided into parameter-based AC (PBAC), measurement-based AC (MBAC), and derivatives thereof. Experience-based AC (EBAC) is one of these derivatives combining both approaches, i.e. PBAC and MBAC, into a new AC concept. LAC methods are usually extended for application in entire networks (cf. Section 3.1.3) for NAC. PBAC offers stringent QoS guarantees to data traffic that has been admitted to the network but it lacks scalability with regard to the signaling of resource reservations. In return, MBAC uses the available network resources very efficiently but relies on real-time traffic measurments and, therefore, it is susceptible to QoS violation.

Parameter-Based AC (PBAC)

Parameter-based AC (PBAC), also known as (a priori) traffic-descriptor-based AC, is an approach appropriate for guaranteed network services [83], i.e., for traffic with stringent QoS requirements. It relies solely on traffic descriptors that are signaled by traffic source or applications and that describe the traffic characteristics of a flow such as peak and mean rate together with token bucket parameters. If an admission request succeeds, bandwidth is reserved and exclusively dedicated to the new flow. As a consequence, PBAC is often inefficient regarding its resource utilization since the traffic descriptors usually overestimate the actual rate to avoid traffic delay and loss due to spacing or policing. With PBAC, traffic is limited either by deterministic worst case considerations like network calculus [84] or by stochastic approaches such as effective bandwidth (cf. Section 3.1.1). PBAC for heterogeneous and variable traffic mixes can lead to very complex calculations.

Measurement-Based AC (MBAC)

Measurement-based AC (MBAC), in contrast, is an AC method adequate for controlled load network services [85], i.e., for traffic with less stringent QoS requirements. It measures the current link or network load in real-time and takes an estimate of the new flow to make the admission decision. The determination of traffic characteristics is thus shifted from a source/application to the network and the source-specified traffic descriptor can be very simple, e.g. the peak rate. MBAC methods presented in literature are either aggregate-oriented or flow-oriented:

- **Aggregate-oriented MBAC (A-MBAC)** Most MBAC approaches measure the traffic properties of the entire traffic aggregate admitted to the link. The effective bandwidths of a flow is only required for the initial admission decision, when the requested bandwidth is compared to the available link capacity. For that purpose, the rate of the admitted traffic aggregate is sufficient. A-MBAC has two advantages. The traffic measurement is simpler as no per flow measurement states have to be managed and the statistical properties of a stationary traffic aggregate are more stable. On the other hand, the admission of new flows and the termination of others make the traffic aggregate a non-stationary process which must be carefully observed [86, 87]. Comparisons of different A-MBAC approaches can be found in [88–94].

- **Flow-oriented MBAC (F-MBAC)** Some MBAC approaches use flow-specific measurements to assess the bandwidth consumption of each traffic flow individually. The initial effective bandwidth of a new flow is calculated based on its declared traffic descriptor. As soon as the confidence in the measurements of an admitted flow is high enough, its effective bandwidth is substituted by an update which is computed based on the measured traffic parameters. Examples of F-MBAC methods are given in [95–98].

All presented MBAC methods use real-time measurements and admit traffic as long as enough capacity is available. The downside of MBAC is its sensitivity to measurement accuracy and its susceptibility to traffic prediction errors which can occur, e.g., during QoS attacks, i.e., when admitted traffic flows are "silent"at the moment and congest the link later by simultaneously sending at high bitrate.

Experience-Based AC (EBAC)

Experience-based AC (EBAC) is the first hybrid AC approach that takes advantage of traffic measurements without real-time requirements. It uses historical information about previously admitted traffic to make current admission decisions. The concept of EBAC is described in detail in Section 3.2 and can be summarized this way: with EBAC, a new flow is admitted to a link at time t if its peak rate together with the peak rates of already admitted flows does not exceed the link capacity multiplied by an overbooking factor $\varphi(t)$. The overbooking factor is calculated based on the reservation utilization of the admitted flows in the past (cf. Section 3.2.3). Hence, this method relies on experience. EBAC also requires traffic measurements to compute the reservation utilization but they do not have real-time requirements and thus influence the admission decision only indirectly. The proof of concept for EBAC is given in Section 3.3 by simulations and corresponding waiting time analyses of the admitted traffic. In particular, EBAC is investigated during steady state for traffic with rather static characteristics. Since MBAC methods are known to be sensitive to traffic variability, we investigate in Section 3.4 the behavior of EBAC in the presence of traffic changes and show its impact on the EBAC-controlled traffic. For what we call conventional EBAC, the overbooking factor $\varphi(t)$ correlates to the average peak-to-mean rate ratio (PMRR) of all admitted traffic flows on the link and only one simple overbooking factor is provided for the entire traffic aggregate. In Section 3.5, we propose a type-specific EBAC which provides a compound overbooking factor for different traffic types subsuming flows with similar PMRRs. The concept can be well implemented since it does not require type-specific traffic measurements. We give a proof of concept for this extension and compare it with the conventional EBAC approach. EBAC can also be extended for resource overbooking within an entire network such that EBAC does not need to be applied link-by-link. In Section 3.6, we show that a border-to-border tunnel-based network architecture fulfills all requirements for an easy network-wide application of EBAC. AC is then performed by admitting flows to virtual border-to-border tunnels. By means of EBAC, these tunnels can be overbooked such that the overal network efficiency is increased while QoS constraints are still met.

3.1.3 Network Admission Control (NAC)

Network admission control (NAC), in contrast to LAC, admits traffic flows for transport through an entire network and not only on a single link. Therefore, NAC must take the paths of flows into account, i.e., it requires information about the routing and load balancing applied in the controlled network. In addition, flows enter the network independently of each other at different ingress routers. This makes NAC a distributed problem. Probe-based NAC (PNAC) methods use distributed instant measurements to decide whether a new flow can be accepted. Budget-based NAC (BNAC) methods perform LAC at different NAC instances that are distributed in the network and dispose of virtual network capacity budgets instead of link capacities.

Probe-Based NAC (PNAC)

Probe-based NAC (PNAC) approaches rely on a status feedback of intermediate routers in the path of a requesting flow. The ingress router of a flow issues probe messages to the destination which are discarded by intermediate routers if the network is overloaded. The overload is diagnosed by local traffic measurements, i.e., if a certain proportion of probes returns, the flow is admitted, otherwise it is rejected. This is the traditional PNAC approach often found in literature [99–104]. The authors of [105], however, abandon the assistance of intermediate routers and perform the acceptance decision based on the normal packet loss ratio that is evaluated by probe messages. A similar implicit approach has been taken to perform AC for TCP traffic [106]. In this case, intermediate routers detect overload and block new TCP flows by discarding their initial SYN packets during their setup phase.

Budget-Based NAC (BNAC)

Budget-based NAC (BNAC) is investigated in detail in [63]. The corresponding AC methods are based on distributed network resource budgets and are differentiated according to their budget types. The budgets have virtual capacities that relate either to specific links, border-to-border (b2b) aggregates, or combinations and sets thereof. They may be used at different NAC locations, e.g., in a central entity, only at the network border routers, or at intermediate core routers. Each flow is associated with a set of resource budgets and it is admitted by BNAC only if AC decisions for all budgets of that set are approved. The individual AC decisions are thereby made according to LAC. The virtual capacity of the budgets must be assigned such that the physical network resources are not unintentionally overbooked and that different b2b aggregates encounter fair flow blocking probabilities. Algorithms for that purpose are also proposed in [63]. The following four BNAC methods can be classified:

- **Link budget-based NAC (LB-NAC)** The LB-NAC is probably the most intuitive BNAC approach. The capacity of each link in the network is managed by a single link budget that may be administered, e.g., at the router sending over that link. A new flow must pass the AC procedure for the budgets of all links that are traversed in the network (cf. Figure 3.1(a)). There are many systems and protocols working according to that principle. CAC in the ATM and the integrated services (IntServ) network architectures adopt it in pure form.

- **Ingress and egress budget-based NAC (IB/EB-NAC)** The IB/EB-NAC defines for every ingress node an ingress budget and for every egress node an egress budget that must not be exceeded. A new flow must pass the AC procedure for both budgets and it is admitted only if both requests are approved (cf. Figure 3.1(b)). Both AC decisions are decoupled, i.e., flows are admitted at their ingress irrespective of their egress router and vice versa. If we omit the egress budgets, we get the simple IB-NAC. This idea fits in the context of differentiated services (DiffServ), where traffic is admitted only at the ingress routers and independent of the destinations of the flows.

- **Border-to-border budget-based NAC (BBB-NAC)** The BBB-NAC takes ingress and egress border router of a flow into account for the AC decision, i.e., a b2b budget manages the capacity of a virtual tunnel between an ingress and an egress router. The tunnels can be implemented, for instance, as label switched paths (LSPs) known from multi-protocol label switching (MPLS) and their capacities may be signaled by corresponding reservation protocols like RSVP-TE or CR-LDP. Figure 3.1(c) illustrates that a new flow passes only a single AC procedure for such a tunnel whose capacity is reserved for one specific b2b aggregate and, therefore, cannot be used for other traffic with different source or destination. The BBB-NAC concept can be implemented in a flexible manner such that the size of a tunnel is adjusted according to the current traffic demands. We call this procedure adaptive bandwidth allocation (ABA) within b2b capacity tunnels and investigate its performance in detail in Chapter 4.

- **Ingress link budget- and egress link budget-based NAC (ILB/ELB-NAC)** The ILB/ELB-NAC defines ingress link budgets and egress link budgets to manage the capacity of each network link. The budgets are administered by border routers and the capacity of each link is partitioned among these routers. The links administered in an ingress router thereby constitute a logical source tree and the links administered by an egress router form a logical sink tree (cf. Figure 3.1(d)). A new flow, entering the network at a specific ingress router and leaving it at a specific egress router, must pass the AC procedure for the respective ingress and egress link budgets of all links traversed in the network. Omitting the egress link budgets makes this BNAC method similar to the hose model [107].

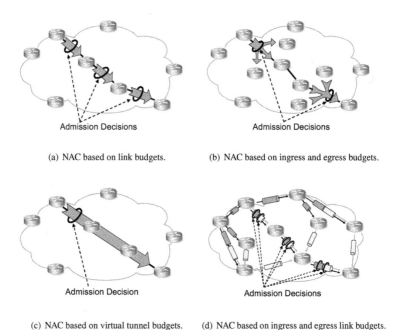

(a) NAC based on link budgets.　　　　(b) NAC based on ingress and egress budgets.

(c) NAC based on virtual tunnel budgets.　　(d) NAC based on ingress and egress link budgets.

Figure 3.1: *Classification of budget-based network admission control (NAC) methods.*

The presented BNAC methods differ in their implementation complexity, their scalability reagarding the reservation state management, and their resource efficiency with and without resilience requirements. More detailed information on the comparison of the BNAC alternatives can be found in [63].

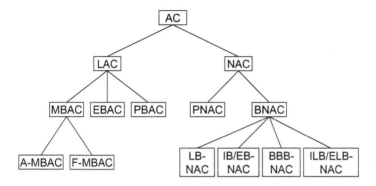

Figure 3.2: *Taxonomy for admission control methods.*

3.1.4 Overview of General AC Methods

Figure 3.2 summarizes our classification of AC methods and gives an overview. Note that this classification does not claim to be complete or exclusive because AC protocols and systems may be classified using different aspects [108]. However, in this work, we primarily distinguish between LAC and NAC. LAC can further be subdivided into MBAC, PBAC, and combined approaches like EBAC. NAC differentiates between PNAC, which is related to MBAC, and BNAC, which is the logic extension of LAC applied to an entire network. EBAC is the main focus of this work and we explain its concept and performance characteristics in this chapter.

3.1.5 Comparison of AC and Capacity Overprovisioning (CO)

Capacity overprovisioning (CO) is an alternative to AC to provision QoS in IP networks. It requires long-term forecasting of Internet traffic [56] and prevents potential overload situations by simply deploying sufficient capacity in the network such that congestions become very unlikely. Therefore, it is easier and cheaper to implement than AC, at least from an OPEX point of view. However, CO requires increased CAPEX for the network infrastructure and cannot exclude pathological traffic patterns, e.g. hot-spot scenarios, in a network without a massive deployment of excess capacity. As a consequence, the resource utilization is very low if CO is applied. AC requires less capacity to protect the QoS of admitted traffic during network congestions since overload traffic can be blocked.

A performance comparison of AC and CO is difficult. One the one hand, many investigations compare blocking probabilities of different AC schemes [109, 110] that are barely used in practice. On the other hand, practical experience shows that CO is already applied in today's core networks [58] though it is not clear how much overcapacity is really needed.

Capacity provisioning fundamentally differs from access to core networks due to the degree of traffic aggregation. For core networks, the traffic on the packet level can be modeled well by the Gaussian distribution [111] due to the high level of aggregation. This is clearly not the case in access networks where the number of individual traffic flows is limited and the aggregation level is inherently low. A comparison of AC and CO for access network dimensioning can be found in [112]. A traffic theoretical approach comparing both concepts with regard to their capacity requirements in the presence of network hot spots is given in [59, 60]. The authors show that a considerable amount of bandwidth can be saved with AC compared to CO if both methods are used to protect against the same unfavorable traffic scenarios. However, they also argue that AC requires a substantial amount of signaling, coordination, and interoperation that is not yet implemented in most networks and that an economic assessment must take this into account.

3.2 Conceptual Design of EBAC and Its Performance Evaluation

Experience-based AC (EBAC) is a hybrid approach combining functional elements of PBAC and MBAC in a novel AC concept. It therefore implements LAC but can be easily extended to a network-wide scope. EBAC relies on peak rate traffic descriptors which may be significantly overestimated in the signaled flow requests. The utilization of the overall reserved capacity gives an estimate for the peak-to-mean rate ratio (PMRR) of the traffic aggregate and allows for the calculation of a factor to overbook the link capacity. The idea is simple but safety margins are required to provide sufficient QoS and questions arise regarding its robustness against variable traffic flows. In this section, we elaborate the EBAC concept [113] and describe its basic functional components [114].

3.2.1 Admission Decision on a Single Link

EBAC makes an admission decision as follows. An AC entity limits the access to a link l with capacity c_l and records the admitted flows $\mathcal{F}(t)$ at any time t together with their requested peak rates $\{r_f : f \in \mathcal{F}(t)\}$. When a new flow f_{new} arrives, it requests for a peak rate $r_{f_{new}}$. If

$$r_{f_{new}} + \sum_{f \in \mathcal{F}(t)} r_f \leq c_l \cdot \varphi(t) \cdot \rho_{max} \qquad (3.1)$$

holds, admission is granted and f_{new} joins $\mathcal{F}(t)$. Otherwise, the new flow request is rejected. Flows are removed from $\mathcal{F}(t)$ on termination. The experience-based overbooking factor $\varphi(t)$ is calculated by statistical analysis and indicates how much more bandwidth than c_l can be safely allocated for reservations. The maximum link utilization threshold ρ_{max} limits the traffic admission such that the expected packet delay W exceeds an upper threshold W_{max} only with probability p_W. The computations of ρ_{max} and $\varphi(t)$ are described in the next sections.

3.2.2 Calculation of the Maximum Link Utilization Threshold

The value of ρ_{max} depends significantly on the traffic characteristics and the capacity c_l of the EBAC-controlled link. Most prominent solutions are based on the $M/M/1 - \infty$ and the $N \cdot D/D/1 - \infty$ queuing system. Real-time traffic produced from, e.g., voice or video applications has a rather constant output rate that can be controlled by a spacer such that a maximum flow rate is enforced. Therefore, we calculate the threshold ρ_{max} based on the $N \cdot D/D/1 - \infty$ approach, which assumes N homogeneous traffic flows in $\mathcal{F}$, each sending packets of constant size B (in bits) and with constant packet inter-arrival times A (in seconds). The mean rate of a flow f is then defined as $c_f = \frac{B}{A}$ and the packet delay distribution of this periodic system is

$$P(W \leq t) = 1 - e^{-2 \cdot x \left(\frac{x}{N} + 1 - \rho \right)}, \qquad (3.2)$$

where $x = \frac{t \cdot c_l}{B}$ and $\rho = \frac{N \cdot c_f}{c_l}$. Equation (3.2) holds provided that $\rho \leq 1$ holds (cf. Section 15.2.4 in [82]). For an inhomogeneous traffic mix $\mathcal{F}$, we use the mean values $E[B]$ and $E[A]$ of the traffic aggregate to compute the distribution. The maximum link utilization threshold ρ_{max} is then

$$\rho_{max} = \max_{\rho} \{ \rho : P(W > W_{max}) \leq p_W \}. \qquad (3.3)$$

Due to Equation (3.2) the maximum link utilization ρ_{max} increases with increasing link capacity c_l and it decreases with increasing packet size B. Table 3.1 shows the resulting ρ_{max} for different link capacities c_l and mean flow rates c_f. The values are calculated for a constant packet size $B = 512$ byte, a maximum delay bound $W_{max} = 5$ ms, and a propability $p_W = 99\%$ to keep this bound. For rather static traffic as simulated in Section 3.3, the mean flow rate c_f is constant and, therefore, ρ_{max} can be calculated according to Equation (3.3). For traffic variations on the packet level as simulated in Section 3.4, the rate c_f is variable.

c_f (Kbit/s)	c_l (Mbit/s)		
	10	100	1000
64	0.8983360	0.99999936	0.999999936
128	0.9720960	0.99999872	0.999999872
256	0.9999616	0.99999744	0.999999744
384	0.9999360	0.99999360	0.999999360
512	0.9999360	0.99999232	0.999999488
768	0.9998592	0.99998976	0.999998976
1536	0.9997824	0.99998208	0.999997440

Table 3.1: *Maximum link utilization threshold ρ_{max} for different link capacities c_l and mean flow rates c_f.*

For the ease of simulation, we then set the maximum link utilization to a conservative and constant value of $\rho_{max} = 0.95$.

The $N \cdot D/D/1 - \infty$ queueing model is merely an approximation for traffic with varying inter-arrival times and packet sizes. However, we will see in Section 3.3 that the adaptive overbooking factor $\varphi(t)$ can compensate the effects of traffic deviations from the exact model.

3.2.3 Calculation of the Overbooking Factor

The overbooking factor $\varphi(t)$ depends on the admitted traffic $\mathcal{F}(t)$ which, in turn, depends on time t because new flows are admitted and existing ones terminate. For the computation of $\varphi(t)$, we define $R(t) = \sum_{f \in \mathcal{F}(t)} r_f$ as the reserved bandwidth of all admitted flows at time t and $C(t)$ denotes their unknown cumulated mean rate. EBAC measures the consumed link bandwidth $M(t)$ of the overall reservation $R(t)$. To obtain $M(t)$, we use equidistant, disjoint interval measurements such that for an interval $I(t_i) = [t_i, t_i + \Delta]$ with length Δ, the measured rate $M(t_i) = \frac{\Gamma(t_i)}{\Delta}$ is determined by metering the traffic volume $\Gamma(t_i)$ sent during $I(t_i)$. For the rates $R(t)$ and $M(t)$, a time statistic for the reservation utilization $U(t) = \frac{M(t)}{R(t)}$ is collected. The values $U(t)$ are sampled in constant time intervals and are stored as hits in bins for a time-dependent histogram $P(t, U)$. From this histogram, the time-dependent p_u-percentile $U_p(t)$ of the empirical distribution of $U(t)$ can be derived as

$$U_p(t) = \min_u \left\{ u : \int_{-\infty}^{u} h(U)dU \geq p_u \right\}, \tag{3.4}$$

where $h(U)$ denotes the probability density function of $U(t)$. Please note that, the histogram $P(t, U)$ discretizes the domain of $U(t)$ and, therefore, Equation (3.4) is actually implemented as a sum. Since traffic characteristics change over time, the reservation utilization statistic must forget obsolete data to reflect the properties of the new traffic mix. Therefore, we record new samples of $U(t)$ by incrementing the corresponding histogram bin by one and devaluate the contents of all histogram bins in regular devaluation intervals I_d by a constant devaluation factor f_d. The devaluation process determines the memory of EBAC which is defined in Section 3.2.4. The reciprocal of the reservation utilization percentile is the overbooking factor

$$\varphi(t) = \frac{1}{U_p(t)} \tag{3.5}$$

which is computed each time, a new value $U(t)$ is put in the histogram. To avoid an underestimation of $U_p(t)$ and an overestimation of $\varphi(t)$, enough statistical data must be collected before Equation (3.5) yields a reliable overbooking factor.

Peak-to-Mean Rate Ratio (PMRR)

The intrinsic idea of EBAC is the exploitation of the peak-to-mean rate ratio (PMRR) of the traffic aggregate admitted to the link. With EBAC, the signaled peak rate r_f of an admitted flow f is enforced by a traffic shaper. In contrast to reality, the mean rate c_f of a flow is known a priori in our simulations. We define the PMRR of a flow by $k_f = \frac{r_f}{c_f}$. Analogously, $K(t) = \frac{R(t)}{C(t)}$ denotes the PMRR of the entire traffic aggregate admitted to the link at time t. $K(t)$ is a natural upper limit for the achievable overbooking factor $\varphi(t)$.

Visualization of Overbooking with EBAC

Figure 3.3 illustrates the principle of EBAC by means of a general example. The development of the reserved bandwidth $R(t)$, the consumed link bandwidth $M(t)$, the PMRR $K(t)$, and the overbooking factor $\varphi(t)$ is indicated over time with and without overbooking by EBAC. The effect of EBAC is clearly visible if we compare the two figures. In Figure 3.3(b), EBAC overbooks the link capacity c_l with reservations $R(t)$ by factor $\varphi(t)$ such that the measured rate $M(t)$ gets closer to the link capacity c_l. This increases the link utilization which EBAC should maximize without exceeding the capacity limit.

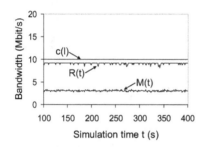

(a) without EBAC overbooking.

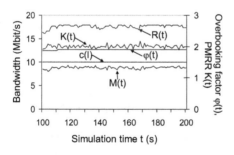

(b) with EBAC overbooking.

Figure 3.3: *Traffic on a single link with and without EBAC overbooking.*

3.2.4 Memory of EBAC

The histogram $P(t, U)$, i.e. the collection and the aging of statistical AC data, implements the memory of EBAC. This memory correlates successive flow admission decisions and consequently influences the adaptation of the overbooking factor $\varphi(t)$ to changing traffic conditions on the link. The statistic aging process, characterized by the devaluation interval I_d and the devaluation factor f_d, makes this memory forget about reservation utilizations in the past. The parameter pairs (I_d, f_d) yield typical half-life periods T_H after which collected values $U(t)$ have lost half of their importance in the histogram. Therefore, we have $\frac{1}{2} = f_d^{T_H/I_d}$ and define the EBAC memory based on its half-life period

$$T_H(I_d, f_d) = I_d \cdot \frac{-ln(2)}{ln(f_d)}. \tag{3.6}$$

With Equation (3.6), different combinations of devaluation parameters (I_d, f_d) and $(I_{d'}, f_{d'})$ yield equal half-life periods if either $I_{d'} = ln(f_{d'})/ln(f_d^{(1/I_d)})$ or $f_{d'} = f_d^{(I_{d'}/I_d)}$ holds. However, these equations guarantee only that the respectively devaluated histograms, assumed that they were equal at a certain time t_0, have aged equally at time $t_1 = t_0 + LCM(I_d, I_{d'})$ where LCM denotes the least common multiple. The reservation utilizations obtained in the interval $[t_0, t_1]$ are experienced differently for the two parameter sets which leads to intermediate deviations between the two histograms and consequently to different overbooking factors.

Time Exponentially-Weighted Moving Histogram (TEWMH)

To express the performance of the EBAC memory by only its characteristic half life period, we introduce the method of time exponentially-weighted moving histogram (TEWMH) [115] which improves the timeliness of the overbooking factor calculation. This method follows the principle of time exponentially-weighted moving average (TEWMA) [116] used to improve the timeliness of rate measurements, and it logically extends TEWMA for application to statistical histograms.

Based on the EBAC memory defined in Equation (3.6), we define the aging rate $a = \frac{ln(f_x)}{I_x}, x \in \{d, d'\}$. Rate a is constant for two parameter sets (I_d, f_d) and $(I_{d'}, f_{d'})$ if they yield the same half-lifeperiod T_H. Instead of incrementing the histogram bins by one, we weight the reservation utilization hits in the time interval $[t_i, t_i + I_x]$ exponentially by the weight factor $\frac{1}{e^{at}}$ and use the result as an increment for the bins. Parameter $t \in [0, I_x - 1]$ thereby denotes the time-offset of the sampled reservation utilization in seconds since the last devaluation. This way, newer values $U(t)$ experienced in the interval $[t_i, t_i + I_x]$ become more important than older values and, as a consequence, all reservation utilizations gathered in this interval are evenly devaluated. In addition, the histograms of both parameter sets are comparable at any time and always lead to identical overbooking factors dependent only on the half-life period T_H.

In Section 3.4.2, the advantage of the TEWMH-based memory implementation of EBAC becomes visible in the presence of traffic changes. There, we compare the overbooking performance of EBAC depending on its memory with and without TEWMH.

3.2.5 EBAC Simulation Design

We evaluate the performance of EBAC on a single link by discrete event simulation. The simulator is implemented in Java^{TM} and based on a simulation library called *JSimLib* which has been developed at the Department of Distributed Systems in the past years.

The design of the simulation is shown in Figure 3.4. Different types of traffic *source generators* produce flow requests that are admitted or rejected by the *admission control* entity. The flows request reservations of different bandwidths which leads to different request-dependent blocking probabilities on a heavily loaded link. To avoid this, we apply trunk reservation [117], i.e., a flow is admitted only if a flow request with maximum reservation size could also be accepted.

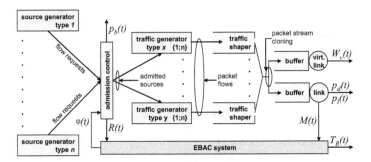

Figure 3.4: *Simulation design for EBAC performance evaluation.*

For an admission decision, the AC entity takes the overbooking factor $\varphi(t)$ into account and admits a flow if Equation (3.5) holds. In turn, the AC entity provides information regarding the reservations $R(t)$ to the *EBAC system* and yields flow blocking probabilities $p_b(t)$. For each admitted source, a *traffic generator* is instantiated to produce a packet flow that is shaped to its contractually defined peak rate. Traffic flows leaving the *traffic shapers* are then multiplexed on the buffered *link* l with capacity c_l. The link provides information regarding the measured traffic $M(t)$ to the EBAC system and yields packet delay probabilities $p_d(t)$ and packet loss probabilities $p_l(t)$.

The performance evaluation of EBAC in steady state (cf. Section 3.3) requires additional effort to investigate the QoS of admitted traffic flows. For this analysis, we clone the traffic streams leaving the shapers and also multiplex them on a *virtual link* l_v with an elastic virtual capacity c_{l_v}. From this link, we then derive a virtual packet delay $W_v(t)$ which serves as a QoS performance measure in our steady-state EBAC simulation. Details on the necessity of this construct are given in Section 3.3.1 The primary performance measure of our non-stationary EBAC simulations is the overall response time T_R, i.e., the time-span required by the EBAC system to fully adapt to a new traffic situation. In Section 3.4, we consider traffic changes on an EBAC-controlled link and evaluate their impact on T_R.

3.2.6 Traffic Models

In our simulations, the traffic controlled by EBAC is modelled on two levels, i.e. the flow scale level and the packet scale level. While the flow level controls the inter-arrival times of flow requests and the holding times of admitted traffic flows, the packet level defines the inter-arrival times and the sizes of packets of individual flows.

Flow Level Model

On the flow level, we distinguish different traffic source types, each associated with a characteristic peak-to-mean rate ratio (PMRR) and corresponding to a source generator type in Figure 3.4. The inter-arrival time of flow requests and the holding time of admitted flows both follow a Poisson model [118], i.e., new flows arrive with rate λ_f and the duration of a flow is controlled by rate μ_f. The mean of the flow inter-arrival time is thus denoted by $1/\lambda_f$ and the holding time of a flow is exponentially distributed with a mean of $1/\mu_f$. Provided that no blocking occurs, the overall offered load $a_f = \frac{\lambda_f}{\mu_f}$ is the average number of simultaneously active flows measured in Erlang. To saturate an EBAC-controlled link with traffic, the load is set to $a_f \geq 1.0$. The latter assumption allows for an evaluation of the EBAC performance under heavy traffic load such that some flow requests are rejected.

Packet Level Model

On the packet level model, we abstract from the wide diversity of packet characteristics induced by the application of different transmission layer protocols. Since we are interested in the basic understanding of the behavior of EBAC, we abstain from real traffic patterns and define a flow of consecutive data packets simply by a packet size distribution and a packet inter-arrival time distribution. Both contribute to the rate variability within a flow that is produced by a traffic generator in Figure 3.4. To keep things simple, we assume a fixed packet size per flow and use a Poisson arrival process to model a packet inter-arrival time ditri-bution with rate λ_p. We are aware of the fact that Poisson is not a suitable model to simulate Internet traffic on the packet level [119]. We therefore generate Pois-son packet streams and subsequentially police the individual flows with peak-rate traffic shapers (cf. Figure 3.4). The properties of the flows are significantly influ-enced by the configuration of these shapers. In practice, the peak rate r_f of a flow f is limited by an application or a network element and the mean rate c_f is often unknown. In our simulations, however, the mean rate is known a priori and, therefore, we can control the rate of flow f by its PMRR $k_f = \frac{r_f}{c_f}$.

Traffic Variations

In Section 3.3, we evaluate the performance of EBAC on a single link carry-ing traffic with rather constant properties on the flow and the packet scale level. Hence, the characteristics of the aggregated traffic on the link remain constant for the entire simulation time. To investigate the robustness of EBAC against traffic variability, we alter the traffic characteristics of admitted flows for different simu-lations. These characteristics are the packet size, the packet inter-arrival time, and correlations thereof. We investigate certain ranges for these parameters and show that EBAC is able to take the differences of the resulting queueing behaviors into account for the calculation of the overbooking factor.

In Section 3.4, the performance of EBAC is studied for traffic changes on the packet scale level. In the corresponding simulations, the PMRRs k_f of admitted flows vary over time which directly impacts the traffic load on the link. We in-vestigate the transient behavior of EBAC through simulation of traffic changes which are characterized by either a decrease or increase of the traffic intensity.

In Section 3.5, we elaborate EBAC for traffic changes on the flow scale level and present an EBAC concept extension which simultaneously improves the over-booking and QoS performance of the system. We assume different traffic types subsuming flows with similar PMRRs and vary their shares in the admitted traffic aggregate, i.e., we keep the traffic characteristics of the individual flows constant and only change their composition on the link.

3.3 Performance of EBAC in Steady State

In this section, we perform steady state simulations of EBAC on a single link carrying traffic with constant properties. We prove the concept of EBAC and show the impact of different measurement time scales and different reservation utilization percentiles on the EBAC system performance. We further show that EBAC is resource efficient and robust against variations of traffic characteristics and that its overbooking performance increases with the link size due to economy of scale. Some of the results are published in [114].

3.3.1 Evaluation Issues of EBAC in Steady-State

Issues on EBAC Performance Evaluation

Our method for evaluating the performance of EBAC in steady state is the following. The objective of AC is to limit packet delay due to queueing and to avoid packet loss due to buffer overflow. If packet loss can be eliminated by sufficiently large buffers, packet delay is the natural performance measure for the assessment of AC mechanisms. If a link is only lightly loaded with traffic, i.e. $C(t) \ll c_l$, the actually experienced packet delay can be very short even for too large overbooking factors like $\varphi(t) \gg K(t)$. Since the overbooking factor must still be reliable if the link is lowly utilized, the packet delay experienced on the admission-controlled link is not suitable for the validation of the EBAC concept. Therefore, we construct another virtual link l_v, load it with clones of the admitted traffic flows (cf. Figure 3.4), and continuously scale down its capacity $c_{l_v}(t)$ such that it is just large enough to meet the QoS requirements of the traffic measured at time t. In doing so, we simulate a virtual link under heavy load which yields a virtual packet delay $W_v(t)$.

We can estimate the mean rate of the admitted traffic by $C(t) = \frac{R(t)}{\varphi(t)}$. We also want to guarantee a maximum packet delay W_{max} on the virtual link with a probability p_W, i.e., $P(W \geq W_{max}) \leq p_W$. Hence, we can compute the time-dependent virtual link capacity $c_{l_v}(t)$, similar to Equation (3.2), based on the $N \cdot D/D/1 - \infty$ queuing system with a mean flow rate c_f as

$$c_{l_v}(t) = min\left(C(t), \ \frac{N \cdot B}{2 \cdot W_{max}} \cdot \left(-1 + \sqrt{1 + \frac{4 \cdot W_{max} \cdot c_f}{B} - \frac{2 \cdot \ln(1 - p_W)}{N}} \right) \right),$$

(3.7)

where $N = \frac{R(t)}{\varphi(t) \cdot c_f}$. Finally, we take the mean $E[W_v]$ of the virtual packet delay $W_v(t)$ and its 99%-percentile $Q_{99}[W_v]$ as measures to quantify the performance of EBAC in steady-state.

Issues on EBAC Simulation Design

We evaluate the performance of EBAC in steady-state through discrete event simulations on a single link. If not mentioned differently, a simulation run is designed as follows: we set up the source generators (cf. Figure 3.4) producing flow requests according to the flow level traffic model and the traffic generators producing packet flows according to the packet level model as described in Section 3.2.6. Each admitted flow request leads to the instantiation of a new traffic generator which, in turn, generates a packet flow with static traffic characteristics and constant PMRR. The simulated link has a capacity of $c_l = 10$ Mbit/s and carries the traffic aggregate composed of all generated and shaped packet flows. A clone of this aggregate is sent to the virtual link l_v. If not mentioned differently, disjoint interval measurements are taken every $\Delta = 1$ s. For every measurement $M(t)$, a reservation utilization sample $U(t)$ is put in the histogram $P(t, U)$ and the overbooking factor $\varphi(t)$ is calculated (cf. Section 3.2.3) with a reservation utilization percentile parameter $p_u = 0.99$. The values for parameters Δ and p_u are chosen with regard to the findings in Section 3.3.3. In parallel, the capacity c_{l_v} of the virtual link is updated and the virtual packet delay W_v is sampled.

3.3.2 Proof of Concept for EBAC

Evidence for the correctness of the EBAC concept is given in [114]. The intrinsic idea of EBAC is the exploitation of the peak-to-mean rate ratio (PMRR) $K(t)$ of the traffic aggregate admitted to the load-controlled link. Therefore, $K(t)$ is a natural upper limit for the achievable overbooking factor $\varphi(t)$ as shown by the following simulations.

Influence of the Average Peak-to-Mean Rate Ratio

We perform multiple simulations with different PMRRs of the admitted traffic aggregate. The traffic flows are homogeneous, i.e., they request bandwidth with a common peak rate of $r_f = 768$ Kbit/s, send packets of constant size $B = 512$ byte, and have the same average PMRR. Each simulation implements the design described in Section 3.3.1.

Figure 3.5(a) illustrates that EBAC adapts the overbooking factor according to the different but constant PMRRs. The average overbooking factor $E[\varphi]$ is almost as large as the average PMRR $E[K]$ of the traffic aggregate. The small deviations result from the link utilization threshold ρ_{max} (cf. Table 3.1 in Section 3.2.2) and the reservation utilization percentile parameter p_u. At the same time, the mean $E[W_v]$ and the 99%-percentile $Q_{99}[W_v]$ of the virtual packet delay W_v are well limited and the QoS of all admitted flows is maintained. To guarantee the statistical significance of our results, we repeat each experiment 10 times and provide the 95% confidence intervals for $E[\varphi]$ and $E[W_v]$ in Figure 3.5(a).

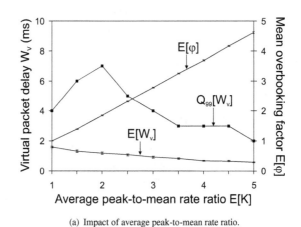

(a) Impact of average peak-to-mean rate ratio.

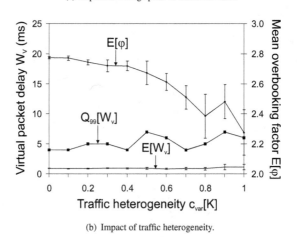

(b) Impact of traffic heterogeneity.

Figure 3.5: *Impact of peak-to-mean rate ratio and traffic heterogeneity on over-booking factor and virtual packet delay.*

Traffic type i	1	2	3
$E[K_i]$	1	3	6
R_i (Kbit/s)	256	768	1536
$E[C_i]$ (Kbit/s)	256	256	256
p_i	$\frac{1}{5} \cdot c_{var}[K]^2$	$1 - \frac{2}{3} \cdot c_{var}[K]^2$	$\frac{4}{15} \cdot c_{var}[K]^2$

Table 3.2: *Traffic type-dependent peak-to-mean rate ratios and their average shares in the admitted traffic mix depending on the traffic heterogeneity parameter $c_{var}[K]$.*

Influence of the Peak-to-Mean Rate Ratio Variability

We release the assumption of homogeneous traffic and use a traffic mix with flows having different PMRRs. In Table 3.2, we distinguish between three different traffic types i, each characterized by its requested peak rate R_i, its actual mean rate C_i, the resulting PMRR K_i, and its occurence probability p_i which depends on the heterogeneity parameter $c_{var}[K] \in \left[0, \sqrt{\frac{3}{2}}\right]$ of the admitted traffic mix. To guarantee fair flow blocking probabilities, we perform trunk reservation. Therefore, the mean rate and the average PMRR of the entire traffic aggregate remains constant in all variations of the traffic mix such that $E[C] = 256$ Kbit/s and $E[K] = 3$.

Figure 3.5(b) shows the performance of EBAC depending on parameter $c_{var}[K]$, i.e. the heterogeneity of the simulated traffic mix. A mean overbooking factor $E[\varphi] < 3$ makes sense as the average PMRR $E[K] = 3$. $E[\varphi]$ decreases with an increasing traffic heterogeneity. Obviously, the EBAC system adapts the overbooking factor φ such that the virtual packet delay W_v is well limited for all variations of the traffic mix. Hence, EBAC also performs well for heterogeneous traffic, though this time, the 95% confidence intervals for the mean overbooking factor are relatively large.

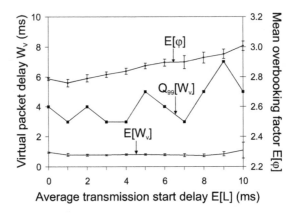

Figure 3.6: *Impact of transmission start delays on overbooking factor and virtual packet delay.*

Influence of the Packet Transmission Start Delay

The start of a packet transmission is usually delayed regarding the admission time of a flow. This is due to signaling and application issues. The delays provoke an underestimated reservation utilization $U(t) = \frac{M(t)}{R(t)}$ since the reserved bandwidth $R(t)$ increases before the packet transmission contributes to the increase of the measured rate $M(t)$. This, in turn, affects the calculation of the overbooking factor $\varphi(t)$.

Figure 3.6 shows the EBAC performance for various transmission start delayes and a simulated traffic aggregate with mean PMRR $E[K] = 3$. The delays have an exponentially distributed latency L which extends the reservation time of an admitted flow by $E[L]$ until its first packets are transmitted. As a consequence of underestimated reservation utilization, we observe that $E[\varphi]$ increases with $E[L]$ and that the virtual packet delay W_v is still under control for moderate transmission start delays.

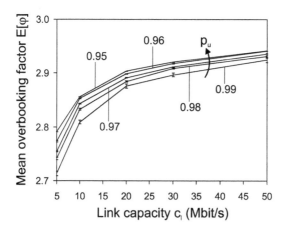

Figure 3.7: *Impact of link capacity and reservation utilization percentile on over-booking factor.*

Influence of the Link Capacity

A series of simulations with different link capacities c_l allows for an investigation of the impact of this parameter on the EBAC overbooking performance. The mean PMRR is again set to $E[K] = 3$. In Figure 3.7, the mean overbooking factor $E[\varphi]$ is shown for different link capacities $c_l \in \{5, 10, 20, 30, 50\}$ Mbit/s and various reservation utilization percentiles $p_u \in [0.95, 0.99]$.

Our results illustrate the phenomenon of economy of scale. Its effect is generally characterized by the fact that a large link allows for a higher resource utilization than a smaller link though both yield the same blocking probability (cf. e.g. [120], pp.93). The economy of scale is reflected by the mean overbooking factor $E[\varphi]$ which increases steadily with the link capacity c_l and thus raises the link utilization. Hence, EBAC takes advantage of higher multiplexing gains that are achievable with larger links. This holds for all settings of parameter p_u.

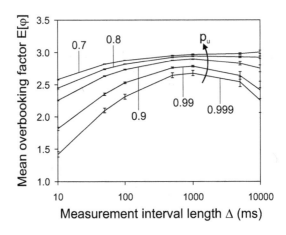

Figure 3.8: *Impact of reservation utilization percentile and measurement interval length on overbooking factor.*

3.3.3 Recommendations for EBAC Parameters

Our experiments with different link capacities show that the value p_u determining the reservation utilization percentile $U_p(t)$ is a critical EBAC parameter that effects the overbooking factor by definition (cf. Equations (3.4) – (3.5)). The measurement interval length Δ is another EBAC parameter with impact on the overbooking and QoS performance of the system. The length of Δ influences significantly the smoothness of the time series of traffic measurements $M(t)$ and thus the distribution of reservation utilizations $U(t) = \frac{M(t)}{R(t)}$ in the histogram $P(t, U)$. To investigate the impact of these two parameters on the EBAC performance measures φ and W_v, we vary p_u from 70% to 99.9% and Δ from 10 ms to 10 s.

Figure 3.8 illustrates the mean overbooking factor $E[\varphi]$ depending on p_u and Δ on a simulated link with capacity $c_l = 10$ Mbit/s. As previously stated, a

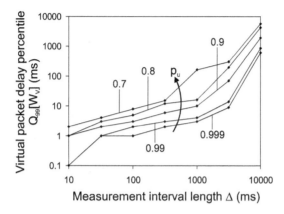

Figure 3.9: *Impact of reservation utilization percentile and measurement interval length on virtual packet delay.*

decreasing value p_u decreases the reservation utilization percentile $U_p(t)$ by definition and, therefore, increases the mean overbooking factor $E[\varphi]$. An increasing measurement interval length Δ reduces the fluctuation of the measured rate $M(t)$ and also that of the utilization $U(t)$. This reduces $U_p(t)$ and increases $E[\varphi]$. However, a stronger traffic concentration on the link due to massive overbooking causes an increment of the virtual packet delay W_v. This can be well observed by its raising 99%-percentile $Q_{99}[W_v]$ in Figure 3.9. The percentile $Q_{99}[W_v]$ is well limited up to a measurement interval of $\Delta = 1$ s and it can be compensated by a more conservative $p_u > 0.9$. For too small values $p_u \leq 0.9$, however, the virtual packet delay is compromised.

For longer intervals Δ, the series of samples $U(t)$ becomes too smooth, the percentile $U_p(t)$ too small, the factor $\varphi(t)$ too large, and the delay W_v too excessive. For a measurement interval $\Delta \approx 10$ s, $E[\varphi]$ shrinks again, though $Q_{99}[W_v]$ continues to increase. A closer look on the simulation data reveals that the coefficient of variation $c_{var}[\varphi]$ of the overbooking factor is about 20 times larger compared to its value for $\Delta = 1$ s, i.e., $\varphi(t)$ is not constant but it fluctuates significantly. By design of the EBAC system, the measurements $M(t)$ are constantly delayed for time Δ, i.e., measurements taken in one interval are used for the computation of $U(t) = \frac{M(t)}{R(t)}$ in the next interval. Hence, flow arrivals and terminations are not reflected timely enough by the values $M(t)$ if Δ is too long.

We conclude that EBAC is not feasible for longer measurement intervals Δ in the magnitude of tens of seconds. A larger percentile parameter p_u assures a conservative overbooking and thereby limits the virtual packet delay W_v. Therefore, we recommend the use of $\Delta = 1$ s and $p_u \in [0.95, 0.99]$ since shorter measurement intervals are difficult to implement with existing hardware and more conservative percentiles are hard to compute with sufficient reliability.

3.3.4 Robustness Against Traffic Variability

The virtual packet delay W_v depends on the virtual link capacity $c_{l_v}(t)$ and the maximum link utilization threshold ρ_{max} which, in turn, depend both on the traffic characteristics of the admitted flows. In particular, the packet size and inter-arrival time distributions as well as correlations thereof are interesting. We investigate parameter ranges for these traffic characteristics and show that EBAC responds well to the different queuing behavior of the simulated traffic by calculating the overbooking factor φ such that it controls the virtual packet delay W_v.

Impact of the Packet Size

According to the $N \cdot D/D/1 - \infty$ queuing formula in Equation (3.2), the packet size B is a key factor for the multiplexing properties of a traffic mix. To investigate the impact of B on the EBAC performance, we conduct multiple simulations with different but constant packet sizes. Figure 3.10(a) shows the mean overbooking factor $E[\varphi]$ and also the mean $E[W_v]$ and the 99%-percentile $Q_{99}[W_v]$ of the virtual packet delay depending on the packet size B. We see that increasing B decreases $E[\varphi]$ such that W_v remains acceptabe. Hence, EBAC can well cope with different packet sizes.

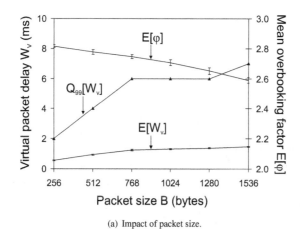

(a) Impact of packet size.

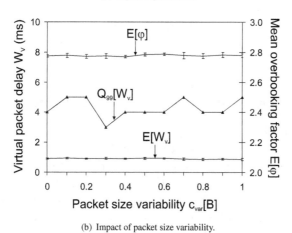

(b) Impact of packet size variability.

Figure 3.10: *Impact of packet size distribution on overbooking factor and virtual packet delay.*

Traffic type i	1	2	3
B_i (bytes)	256	512	1536
p_i	$4 \cdot \frac{c_{var}[B]^2}{5}$	$1 - c_{var}[B]^2$	$\frac{c_{var}[B]^2}{5}$

Table 3.3: *Packet size distributions for different packet size variabilities $c_{var}[B]$.*

Impact of the Packet Size Variability

We drop the assumption of homogeneous traffic with single-sized packets and consider traffic mixes with flows of different types i. Each traffic type i is characterized by its packet size B_i and its occurence probability p_i. The parametrization of the packet size distribution in Table 3.3 allows for $c_{var}[B] \in [0, 1]$.

Figure 3.10(b) shows the mean overbooking factor $E[\varphi]$, the mean virtual packet delay $E[W_v]$, and the 99%-percentile $Q_{99}[W_v]$ for different packet size variabilities $c_{var}[B]$. The value of $c_{var}[B]$ has no visible impact, neither on $E[\varphi]$ nor on $E[W_v]$ and $Q_{99}[W_v]$. Hence, EBAC is robust against different packet size distributions.

Impact of the Packet Inter-Arrival Time Variability

We implicitly investigated the average packet inter-arrival time $E[A]$ by studying the impact of the packet size B earlier in this section. The results allow for the conclusion that EBAC also copes well with different means of the packet inter-arrival time. We now study the impact of the packet inter-arrival time variability $c_{var}[A]$ by using Erlang-k ($c_{var}[A] \in \left]0, 1\right]$) and hyper-exponential ($c_{var}[A] \in \left]1, 2\right]$) distributions for A within a single flow. According to Figure 3.11, the mean overbooking factor $E[\varphi]$ is only slightly reduced for increasing packet inter-arrival time variabilities. At the same time, the mean $E[W_v]$ of the virtual packet delay hardly increases whereas its 99%-percentile $Q_{99}[W_v]$ increases considerably. However, for a reasonable and non-conservative assump-

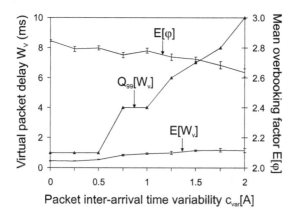

Figure 3.11: *Impact of packet inter-arrival time variability on overbooking factor and virtual packet delay.*

tion of $c_{var}[A] = 1$, tolerable values for $Q_{99}[W_v] \approx 4$ ms are still accomplished. Hence, EBAC copes also well with flows having clearly different packet inter-arrival time distributions.

Impact of Traffic Correlations

Correlations of consecutive packet inter-arrival times have strong impact on the queuing behavior of individual traffic flows. To show the impact of traffic correlations on the performance of EBAC, we use a simple model for correlated traffic. Each traffic source has two discrete Markov states s_0 (off) and s_1 (on). In on state, a source sends packets according to the corresponding packet inter-arrival time distribution whereas in off state, the sending of packets is suppressed. At the end of an inter-arrival time, the state of a source changes from s_i to s_j with probability p_{ij}. The probability that a source is in state s_1 is $p_1 = \frac{p_{01}}{1-p_{11}+p_{01}}$. The transition probability p_{11} is used to control the average burst length $E[L_{burst}] = \frac{1}{1-p_{11}}$

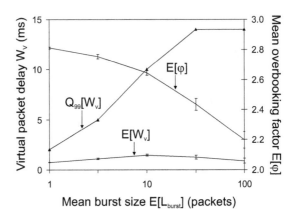

Figure 3.12: *Impact of traffic correlations on overbooking factor and virtual packet delay.*

in packets. We set the state probability $p_1 = 0.5$, which leads to transition probabilities $p_{00} = p_{11} = \frac{(1-p_{11}) \cdot p_1}{1-p_1}$ and $p_{01} = p_{10} = 1 - p_{11}$. The average packet inter-arrival time is set to $E[A] = \frac{B}{2 \cdot E[C]}$ to achieve a mean aggregate rate $E[C]$. The simulated traffic mix is homogeneous and the corresponding flows send packets of constant size $B = 512$ bytes.

Figure 3.12 illustrates the performance of EBAC for traffic with different inter-arrival time correlations indicated by the average burst length $E[L_{burst}]$ in packets. EBAC reduces the overbooking factor $E[\varphi]$ significantly for an increasing burstiness of the traffic. This way, the 99%-percentile of the virtual packet delay is well limited to $Q_{99}[W_v] \approx 10$ ms for moderately correlated traffic ($E[L_{burst}] = 10$ packets). Strong burstiness of the traffic leads to long periods for which the traffic is sent with twice the mean aggregate rate. For instance, a mean burst length of $E[L_{burst}] = 100$ packets takes about 1.6 s and is sent with a rate of $2 \cdot E[C]$ Kbit/s. Even for this extreme case, the mean virtual packet delay is very low ($E[W_v] \approx 1$ ms) and only its 99%-percentile is slightly increased

$(Q_{99}[W_v] \approx 13 \text{ ms})$. Hence, EBAC is able to cope with strongly correlated traffic and, therefore, proves to be robust against all kinds of traffic variability.

Summary

We have illustrated the performance of EBAC in steady state, i.e. for traffic with almost constant properties. The overbooking factor $\varphi(t)$ primarily depends on the peak-to-mean rate ratio $K(t)$ of the admitted traffic aggregate and decreases with an increasing heterogeneity of the traffic. The impact of transmission start delays of admitted traffic flows on $\varphi(t)$ is negligible and diminishes for a large number of flows. EBAC benefits from the economy of scale and, therefore, provides larger overbooking factors on links with higher capacities. The calculation of $\varphi(t)$ is significantly influenced by the settings of the EBAC system parameters such as the applied reservation utilization percentile p_u and measurement interval length Δ. Simulation results show that a utilization percentile $p_u \in [0.95, 0.99]$ and a measurement interval length $\Delta = 1$ s work well on a 10 Mbit/s link. Increasing the variability of the admitted traffic aggregate causes EBAC to lower the overbooking factor such that the QoS is maintained. The latter also depends on the maximum link utilization threshold ρ_{max} and can be measured by the virtual packet delay W_v. Further simulation experiments prove that EBAC is adaptive such that QoS can be guaranteed even for traffic with high variability and burstiness. The primary objectives of EBAC are always met, i.e., almost the peak-to-mean ratio is used for overbooking such that the resource utilization is increased while the QoS is maintained.

3.4 Performance of EBAC in the Presence of Traffic Changes

The previous section investigated the performance of EBAC through steady state simulation on a single link carrying traffic with constant properties. This section discusses the transient behavior of EBAC in the presence of traffic changes, i.e., when the traffic characteristics of the EBAC-controlled flows change. We investigate the response time T_R required by the EBAC system to provide a new appropriate overbooking factor $\varphi(t)$ after a decrease or increase of the traffic intensity. We consider sudden changes of the traffic characteristics to have worst case scenarios and to obtain upper bounds on T_R. We simulate them with only two types of traffic flows since only the properties of the entire admitted traffic aggegate are of interest for the calculation of $\varphi(t)$. The simulations allow for an examination of the memory from which EBAC gains its experience and which influences the behavior of EBAC in both stationary and non-stationary state. Our results show that the transient behavior of EBAC partly depends on its adjustable memory and that EBAC copes well with even strongly changing traffic characteristics. Some of the results are published in [121].

3.4.1 Evaluation Issues of EBAC in Transient State

For the performance evaluation of EBAC in case of traffic changes, we use a simulation design similar to Figure 3.4. However, we can omit the virtual link l_v since, this time, EBAC is simulated under heavy traffic load, i.e., we saturate the EBAC-controlled link with flow requests. To achieve traffic saturation, we set the traffic characteristics $\lambda_f = \frac{1}{750 \text{ ms}}$ and $\mu_f = \frac{1}{90 \text{ s}}$ on the flow level of the traffic model. Therefore, an overestimation of the overbooking factor due to an underutilization of the link l as described in Section 3.3.1 is impossible and the packet delay W is directly taken from link l. For all simulations, we use a link capacity of $c_l = 10$ Mbit/s, a reservation utilization percentile $p_u = 0.99$, and a measurement interval $\Delta = 1$ s.

The primary performance measure of our non-stationary EBAC simulations is the overall response time T_R, i.e., the time span required by the EBAC system to fully adapt the overbooking factor $\varphi(t)$ to a new traffic situation. We evaluate T_R for different settings of the EBAC memory T_H which depends on the histogram devaluation interval I_d and the devaluation factor f_d. We use the time exponentially-weighted moving histogram (TEWMH) method described in Section 3.2.4 to avoid multiple simulations for different parameter combinations (I_d, f_d) yielding the same half-life period T_H (cf. Equation (3.6)). We use the packet delay W obtained from link l to derive time-dependent packet delay probabilities $p_d(t)$. Together with the time-dependent flow blocking probabilities $p_b(t)$ determined by the admission control process, they serve as indicators for potential QoS degradation.

The change of the traffic intensity is achieved by simultaneously adjusting the rates of all active flows in the simulation. The flow rates are controlled on the packet level of the traffic model by the setting of rate λ_p for the packet inter-arrival time distribution. Increasing λ_p thereby decreases the rate of a flow and vice versa.

3.4.2 Decrease of the Traffic Intensity

We first investigate the change of the traffic intensity from a high to a low value which corresponds to an increase of the peak-to-mean rate ratio (PMRR) $K(t)$ of the simulated traffic under control of EBAC.

Slow Decrease of the Traffic Intensity

We start with a slow decrease of the traffic intensity and thereby show the advantage of the TEWMH over the conventional histogram method. The former uses adaptive increments as calculated in Section 3.2.4 while the latter uses simple increments of constant size 1 to indicate a hit in the reservation utilization histogram $P(t, U)$. The content of $P(t, U)$ controls the overbooking factor $\varphi(t)$.

In our simulation, the traffic intensity, i.e., the PMRR of the simulated flows is controlled by the rate function $\lambda_p(t)$ for the packet inter-arrival time distribution:

$$\lambda_p(t) = \begin{cases} \lambda_p^0 & \text{for } t \leq t_0 \\ \lambda_p^0 + \frac{t-t_0}{t_1-t_0} \cdot (\lambda_p^1 - \lambda_p^0) & \text{for } t_0 < t < t_1 \\ \lambda_p^1 & \text{for } t \geq t_1. \end{cases} \qquad (3.8)$$

Equation (3.8) defines a linear decrease of the traffic intensity that starts at time t_0 with rate λ_p^0 and ends at time t_1 with rate λ_p^1. A traffic intensity decrease corresponds to an increase of the PMRR $K(t)$ as illustrated in Figures 3.13(a) and 3.13(b). At simulation time $t_0 = 230$ s, the PMRR starts to increase from $K(t) = 2$ to $K(t) = 4$ at $t_1 = 590$ s, i.e., all traffic sources slow down and the rates of the generated packet flows are steadily reduced. Figures 3.13(a) and 3.13(b) show simulation results averaged over 50 runs for different combinations of histogram devaluation intervals I_d and devaluation factors f_d which yield equal half-life periods of $T_H = 20$ s.

For a small devaluation interval $I_d = 10$ s in Figure 3.13(a), the development of the overbooking factor (OBF) $\varphi(t)$ is rather smooth. At time $t_0 = 230$ s, the measured rate $M(t)$ decreases according to the traffic reduction. With a certain delay, EBAC increases $\varphi(t)$ and, therefore, more flows are accepted such that the reserved rate $R(t)$ is rising and $M(t)$ increases again to almost its former level.

For a long devaluation interval $I_d = 360$ s in Figure 3.13(b), the development of $\varphi(t)$ equals a step function. At time $t = 230$ s, $M(t)$ starts to decrease as before. At time $t = 360$ s, EBAC devaluates the contents of the histogram $P(t, U)$ for the first time and strongly increases $\varphi(t)$ according to the changed traffic situation. In a short period of time, a large number of new flows are admitted by EBAC and $R(t)$ rises quickly. For the next 360 s, $\varphi(t)$ remains rather constant although the traffic intensity is still decreasing. Hence, $M(t)$ decreases again. At time $t = 720$ s, $P(t, U)$ is devaluated once more, and $\varphi(t)$ and $R(t)$ increase suddenly as for the last devaluation. Finally, the EBAC system reaches a new stable state after the decrease of the traffic intensity is finished.

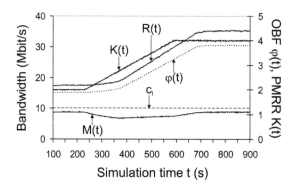

(a) Smooth function $\varphi(t)$ for devaluation interval $I_d = 10$ s and devaluation factor $f_d = 0.707$.

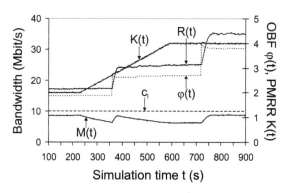

(b) Stepwise function $\varphi(t)$ for devaluation interval $I_d = 360$ s and devaluation factor $f_d = 3.815 \cdot 10^{-6}$.

Figure 3.13: *Impact of different combinations of histogram devaluation parameters with equal half-life period $T_H = 20$ s on overbooking factor.*

The stepwise development of $\varphi(t)$ in Figure 3.13(b) is due to the fact that at times of devaluation, the contents of the reservation utilization histogram $P(t, U)$ are strongly devaluated by factor $f_d = 3.815 \cdot 10^{-6}$ such that the bins in $P(t, U)$ are almost empty. Therefore, each new sample $U(t)$ in $P(t, U)$ that enters shortly after a devaluation has a strong effect on the reservation utilization percentile $U_p(t)$ and, hence, on $\varphi(t) = \frac{1}{U_p(t)}$. As a consequence, the steps of $\varphi(t)$ are determined by the current reservation utilization $U(t) = \frac{M(t)}{R(t)}$ at times t of devaluation. At these time instants, the corners of the steps of $\varphi(t)$ approach the PMRR $K(t)$ and there is no safety margin between them anymore which may lead to QoS violations. After the first devaluation, the utilizations $U(t)$ inserted into $P(t, U)$ decrease since $R(t)$ increases quickly and $M(t)$ continues to decrease. The 99%-percentile $U_p(t)$ thereby decreases only very slowly which keeps $\varphi(t)$ on a rather constant level until the next devaluation.

We replace the conventional histogram by a time exponentially-weighted moving histogram (TEWMH) to avoid the step function for $\varphi(t)$. With TEWMH, all combinations (I_d, f_d) yielding a half-life period $T_H = 20$ s lead to the same smooth development of $\varphi(t)$ as in Figure 3.13(a). Instead of incrementing the bins in $P(t, U)$ by one, we add weighted increments that give more importance to newer reservation utilization values (cf. Section 3.2.4). The samples $U(t)$ are thus evenly devaluated.

The simulation results for an extended set of EBAC memory parameters with $T_H(I_d, f_d) = 20$ s are summarized in Table 3.4 for the conventional (CONV) and the TEWMH method. The average link utilization $E[U_l] = \text{avg}_t\{\frac{c_l}{M(t)}\}$ and the minimum deviation $\delta_{min} = \min_t\{K(t) - \varphi(t)\}$ for $t \in [200\ s, 800\ s]$ assess the performance of both approaches. For the CONV method, $E[U_l]$ decreases for large values of I_d which is disadvantageous in a situation where traffic is blocked. Increasing I_d also reduces the safety margin between $\varphi(t)$ and its natural upper limit $K(t)$. For $I_d = 310$ s and $I_d = 360$ s we have $\delta_{min} < 0$ and, therefore, the QoS of admitted traffic is jeopardized for too long devaluation intervals. In contrast, applying the TEWMH method provides rather constant values $E[U_l]$ and δ_{min}, regardless of the settings of I_d and f_d.

I_d (s)	f_d	$E[U_l]$		δ_{min}	
		CONV	TEWMH	CONV	TEWMH
10	0.707	0.781	0.781	0.096	0.087
60	0.125	0.780	0.781	0.096	0.095
110	$2.209 \cdot 10^{-2}$	0.773	0.780	0.086	0.097
160	$3.906 \cdot 10^{-3}$	0.790	0.782	0.096	0.089
210	$6.905 \cdot 10^{-4}$	0.778	0.781	0.047	0.088
260	$1.221 \cdot 10^{-4}$	0.764	0.781	0.073	0.092
310	$2.158 \cdot 10^{-5}$	0.756	0.780	-0.002	0.097
360	$3.815 \cdot 10^{-6}$	0.720	0.781	-0.002	0.089

Table 3.4: *Mean link utilization $E[U_l]$ and minimum overbooking factor deviation δ_{min} for a slow traffic intensity decrease and different EBAC memory parameters with constant $T_H(I_d, f_d) = 20$ s.*

In summary, the presented results show that the conventional histogram method is well applicable, but it must be carefully parameterized, i.e., its devaluation interval I_d must not be chosen too long compared to the half-life period T_H. Very short intervals increase the computational overhead for the devaluation of the histogram. The TEWMH is preferable since it does not require any other parameters besides the half-life period T_H. Its percentile $U_p(t)$ reacts rather quickly even for long devaluation intervals I_d. This improves the timeliness of the histogram without sacrificing the statistical significance of its values. Therefore, TEWMH is our preferred method for the implementation of the EBAC memory and it is used for all further simulations.

Sudden Decrease of the Traffic Intensity

We now investigate a sudden decrease of the traffic intensity, i.e., all currently and future admitted traffic sources simultaneously reduce their sending rate from one moment to the next. The simulation is designed similar to the slow traffic intensity decrease and the TEWMH method is again used to implement the

EBAC memory. At simulation time $t_0 = 250$ s, the PMRR suddenly increases from $K(t) = 2$ to $K(t) = 3$.

Figures 3.14(a) and 3.14(b) illustrate simulations averaged over 50 runs for different EBAC memories with half-life periods $T_H = 20$ s and $T_H = 60$ s. The primary y-axis indicates the link capacity c_l, the overall reserved bandwidth $R(t)$, and the consumed link bandwidth $M(t)$. The sudden increase of the PMRR results in an immediate decrease of $M(t)$ which also decreases the reservation utilization $U(t) = \frac{M(t)}{R(t)}$. Over time, the histogram $P(t, U)$ collects more and more low utilization values. As a consequence, the 99%-percentile $U_p(t)$ decreases which leads to a higher overbooking factor (OBF) $\varphi(t) = \frac{1}{U_p(t)}$. Hence, more traffic sources are admitted to the link and the reserved rate $R(t)$ rises. Finally, the EBAC system stabilizes again with an expected overbooking factor $\varphi(t) \approx 3$. The speed of the adaptation process is obviously influenced by the EBAC memory parameter T_H.

To measure the duration of the transient phase, i.e., the time until the overbooking factor reaches a new stable value, we calculate the difference between the PMRR $K(t)$ and the overbooking value $\varphi(t)$. If $K(t) - \varphi(t) < \varepsilon$, the transition between the two traffic scenarios is completed and the EBAC system is in steady state again. We therefore define the EBAC response time

$$T_R = \min \{t_i - t_0 : K(t_i) - \varphi(t_i) < \varepsilon \wedge t_i > t_0\} \qquad (3.9)$$

and set the threshold $\varepsilon = 0.2$ in our simulations. This value is specific to our experiments and seems to be appropriate with regard to the asymptotic convergence of $\varphi(t)$ to $K(t)$. Using the TEWMH method for the EBAC memory, $\varphi(t) \leq K(t)$ always holds. The statistical significance of our results is assured by calculating the 95% confidence intervals of the overbooking factor $\varphi(t)$ within 50 iterations of the simulation. As a result, the confidence intervals turn out to be so narrow that we omit them in Figures 3.14(a) and 3.14(b) for the sake of clarity.

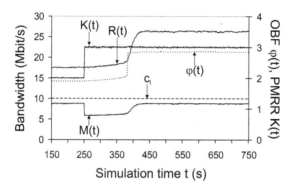

(a) EBAC memory with half-life period $T_H = 20$ s.

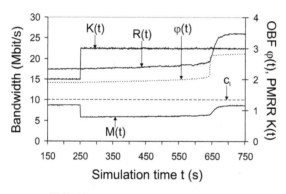

(b) EBAC memory with half-life period $T_H = 60$ s.

Figure 3.14: *Impact of different EBAC memory half-life periods on time-dependent overbooking factor.*

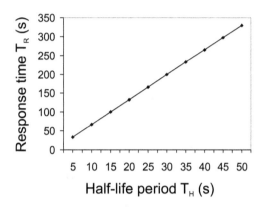

Figure 3.15: *Correlation between half-life period of EBAC memory and EBAC response time for decreasing traffic intensity.*

The different progressions of the overbooking factor $\varphi(t)$ in Figures 3.14(a) and 3.14(b) show that for a sudden traffic intensity decrease, the EBAC response time T_R strongly depends on the EBAC memory represented by the half-life period T_H. To investigate the correlation between T_R and T_H, we perform a series of experiments with varying half-life periods and measure the EBAC response times. Figure 3.15 shows that there is an almost linear dependency between the EBAC response time T_R and the half-life period T_H of the EBAC memory.

3.4.3 Increase of the Traffic Intensity

We now change the traffic intensity from a low to a high value which corresponds to a decrease of the aggregate PMRR $K(t)$, i.e., all admitted and future traffic sources simultaneously raise their sending rate from one moment to the next. This corresponds to a collaborative QoS attack. In contrast to the previous experiment, the QoS is at risk here as the link suddenly gets overloaded and the packet delay and flow blocking probabilities increase as expected during a QoS attack. To blind out the impact of the link buffer (cf. Figure 3.4) on the EBAC response time, we set its value to infinity. The QoS attack experiment is designed analogous to the decrease of the traffic intensity, but the sending rates of all traffic sources are increased such that the PMRR decreases from $K(t) = 3$ to $K(t) = 2$.

Figures 3.16(a) and 3.16(b) show the overbooking and QoS performance of EBAC for a short half-life period of $T_H = 5.76$ s while Figures 3.17(a) and 3.17(b) show the same results for $T_H = 65.79$ s. At time $t_0 = 250$ ms, the QoS attack starts. As the link becomes overutilized, the fill level of the link buffer increases and the packet delay probability $p_d(t) = P(\text{packet delay} > 50 \text{ ms})$ and the flow blocking probability $p_b(t)$ raise to 100% (cf. Figures 3.16(b) and 3.17(b)). As another consequence, the overbooking factor (OBF) $\varphi(t)$ decreases due to a rising reservation utilization percentile $U_p(t)$ and all new flows are blocked by EBAC. Over time, some admitted flows expire and their reserved bandwidth is released. However, the overbooking factor $\varphi(t)$ is further decreased as long as the packet delay and the link load are high. Hence, the overbooking factor decreases below its target value of $\varphi(t) \approx 2$ (cf. Figures 3.16(a) and 3.17(a)). When enough flows have expired, the link buffer empties and the QoS is restored as a result of the decreased overbooking factor. Figures 3.16(b) and 3.17(b) show that the time T_R^Q required to restore QoS is almost the same for the short and the long EBAC memory, respectively. After a certain time span T_R^U, the overestimated reservation utilizations in the histogram are faded out by statistic aging. Simultaneously, the overbooking factor $\varphi(t)$ and the link utilization $U_l(t)$ converge to stable values when the EBAC system reaches its steady state again.

In contrast to Equation (3.9), we now define the EBAC response time as

$$T_R = T_R^Q + T_R^U, \tag{3.10}$$

where $T_R^Q = \min \{t_i - t_0 : p_d(t_i) = 0 \wedge t_i > t_0\}$ is the QoS restoration time and $T_R^U = \min\{t_j - (t_0 + T_R^Q) : K(t_i) - \varphi(t_i) < \varepsilon \wedge t_j > t_0 + T_R^Q\}$ is the utilization restoration time.

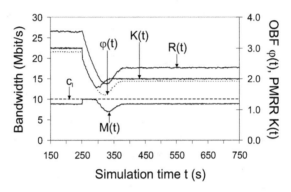

(a) Overbooking performance.

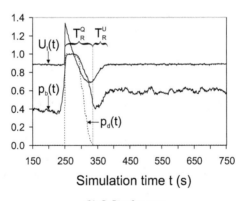

(b) QoS performance.

Figure 3.16: *Time-dependant EBAC performance during a QoS attack for an EBAC memory with half-life period $T_H = 5.76$ s.*

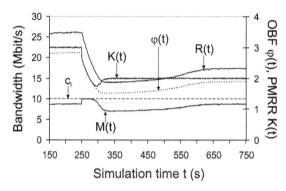

(a) Overbooking performance.

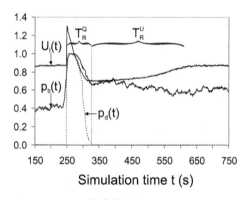

(b) QoS performance.

Figure 3.17: *Time-dependant EBAC performance during a QoS attack for an EBAC memory with half-life period $T_H = 65.79$ s.*

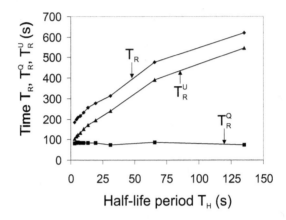

Figure 3.18: *Impact of EBAC memory half-life period on overall response time and QoS/utilization restoration times of EBAC.*

We simulate a sudden traffic intensity increase for various half-life periods T_H of the EBAC memory. Our simulation results compiled in Figure 3.18 show that T_H influences the overall response time T_R of EBAC after a QoS attack. However, it does not influence the time T_R^Q that is required to restore the QoS.

For the sake of completeness, we perform further experiments to investigate the impact of the mean flow holding time $E[1/\mu_f]$, the link buffer size B, and the link capacity c_l on the behavior of EBAC in case of a QoS attack. Table 3.5 shows that larger values for $E[1/\mu_f]$ and B both extend the EBAC response time T_R. However, increasing the mean flow holding time $E[1/\mu_f]$ primarily extends the QoS restoration time T_R^Q. This is reasonable since the restoration of QoS requires the termination of some admitted flows which are active on average for a longer time. Increasing the link buffer size B affects particularly the utilization restoration time T_R^U. A large buffer requires a longer time to be emptied. Therefore, the measured rate $M(t)$ is kept high for a longer time, more overesti-

$E[1/\mu_f]$ (s)	60	90	120	90		
B (ms)		1000		500	1000	2000
T_R (s)	105	119	132	70	118	143
T_R^Q (s)	45	62	77	54	62	64
T_R^U (s)	60	57	55	16	56	79

Table 3.5: *Impact of mean flow holding time $E[1/\mu_f]$ and buffer size B on compound EBAC response time $T_R = T_R^Q + T_R^U$ for half-life period $T_H = 20$ s.*

mated reservation utilizations $U(t)$ are sampled into the histogram $P(t, U)$, and a longer time T_R^U is required to fade them out.

Figures 3.19(a) and 3.19(b) illustrate the overbooking and the QoS performance of EBAC during a sudden increase of the traffic intensity on a link with capacity $c_l = 100$ Mbit/s. The EBAC memory is set to $T_H = 65.79$ s and, therefore, the results are directly comparable to Figures 3.17(a) and 3.17(b). The link capacity c_l has no remarkable effect on the overall EBAC response time T_R or its components T_R^Q and T_R^U. The temporary underestimation of $\varphi(t)$ and, hence, the end of the transient phase of the overbooking adaptation are clearly more visible on the link with capacity $c_l = 100$ Mbit/s. This is due to the large number of flows that are multiplexed on the link and that allow for a more precise overbooking of the link resources.

The above statements concerning the impact of the mean flow holding time $E[1/\mu_f]$, the buffer size B, and the link capacity c_l hold for arbitrary settings of the EBAC memory parameter T_H.

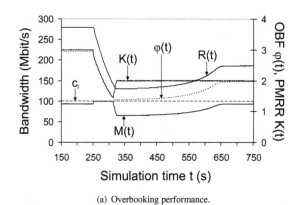

(a) Overbooking performance.

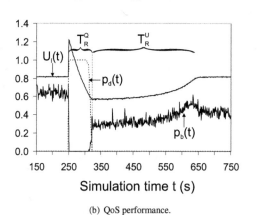

(b) QoS performance.

Figure 3.19: *Time-dependant EBAC performance during a QoS attack for a 100 Mbit/s link and an EBAC memory with half-life period of $T_H = 65.79$ s.*

Summary

We have illustrated the performance of EBAC in the presence of traffic changes, i.e. for a decrease and an increase of the traffic intensity. The traffic changes are simulated by corresponding changes of the peak-to-mean rate ratio of the entire traffic aggregate. EBAC partly relies on traffic measurements and, therefore, it is susceptible to changes of the traffic characteristics of the admitted traffic aggregate. EBAC forgets about old measurements due to its limited memory that is defined by its half-life period T_H. The EBAC memory is implemented by devaluating the reservation utilization histogram $P(t, U)$ in regular intervals I_d with a factor $f_d \leq 1$. Using a time exponentially-weighted moving histogram (TEWMH) makes the devaluation process independent of different parameter pairs (I_d, f_d) yielding the same half-life period T_H. TEWMH is thus the preferred method for the implementation of the EBAC memory. A slow decrease of the traffic intensity reveals its advantage compared to the conventional histogram approach. For a suddenly decreasing traffic intensity, the overall EBAC response time T_R required to adapt the overbooking factor $\varphi(t)$ to the new traffic situation depends linearly on the half-life period T_H. In this case, the QoS of admitted traffic flows is not at risk. For a suddenly increasing traffic intensity, however, the QoS is compromised for a certain time. The overall EBAC response time is then split into two time components $T_R = T_R^Q + T_R^U$ where T_R^Q is the QoS restoration time and T_R^U is utilization restoration time. For a QoS attack, T_R^U depends on the half-life period T_H whereas T_R^Q is independent of it. Longer mean flow holding times and larger link buffers have an elongating impact on T_H. The former mainly influences T_R^Q whereas the latter primarily affects T_R^U. Larger link capacities have no visible effect on T_H, but the reaction of the EBAC system facing a QoS attack is stronger.

3.5 EBAC with Type-Specific Overbooking (TSOB)

In the previous sections, the performance of EBAC is investigated for constant traffic and for traffic changes in terms of decreasing or increasing traffic intensity of individual flows. For the calculation of the overbooking factor $\varphi(t)$, only the traffic characteristics of the entire aggregate of admitted flows are considered. We now propose EBAC with type-specific overbooking (TSOB) which extends the original EBAC concept. EBAC with TSOB uses additional information about the characteristics of individual traffic types and about the composition of admitted traffic to calculate a compound overbooking factor $\varphi_c(t)$. We therefore consider different traffic types subsuming flows with similar peak-to-mean rate ratio and also their share in the currently admitted traffic mix. The concept of TSOB improves EBAC and can be well implemented since it does not require type-specific traffic measurements. This section gives a proof of concept for EBAC with TSOB. We describe the system extension, show how the compound overbooking factor $\varphi_c(t)$ can be calculated without type-specific traffic measurements, and compare EBAC with TSOB to conventional EBAC. The simulation results show that EBAC with TSOB leads to better resource utilization under normal conditions and to faster response times for changing traffic mixes. Some of the results are published in [122].

3.5.1 Evaluation Issues of EBAC with TSOB

For the performance evaluation of EBAC with TSOB, we use the simulation setup described in Section 3.4.1. However, the EBAC-controlled link is now saturated with flow requests of different types of traffic. For the ease of presentation, we simulate with only two traffic types $i \in \{1, 2\}$ whose individual traffic characteristics are shown in Table 3.6.

A comparison of EBAC with TSOB and conventional EBAC regards the responsiveness of the two systems to traffic changes on the link. A good respon-

Traffic type i	1	2
$E[K_i]$	8	2
R_i (Kbit/s)	768	768
$E[C_i]$ (Kbit/s)	96	384
$E[1/\mu_{f_i}]$ (s)	90	90
$E[A_i]$ (ms)	865	3460
$E[\alpha_1]$	0.8	0.2

Table 3.6: *Traffic characteristics of simulated traffic types.*

siveness leads to a high and stable link utilization and simultaneously avoids excessive packet delay. Therefore, we take the mean $E[U_l]$ and the coefficient of variation $c_{var}[U_l]$ of the link utilization U_l and also the packet delay probability p_d as performance measures.

Changes of the traffic intensity are now due to changes of the traffix mix. The rates of individual flows remain constant subject only to statistical fluctuations on the packet scale level of the traffic model. The shares $\alpha_i(t)$ of the traffic types i in the traffic mix are controlled on the flow scale level by setting the mean type-specific flow request inter-arrival times $E[1/\lambda_{f_i}]$. Increasing $E[1/\lambda_{f_i}]$ thereby decreases the share of traffic type i in the traffic mix.

3.5.2 EBAC System Extension for TSOB

We assume that different applications produce traffic flows with typical peak-to-mean rate ratios (PMRRs) $K_i(t)$ which lead to different type-specific overbooking factors $\varphi_i(t)$. Parameter i then denotes a traffic type subsuming flows of different applications but with similar PMRRs K_i. The EBAC admission decision for a new flow f_i^{new} of type i is then extended to

$$r_{f_i^{new}} \cdot U_{p,i}(t) + \sum_{f \in \mathcal{F}(t)} r_f \cdot U_{p,type(f)}(t) \leq c_l \cdot \rho_{max}. \quad (3.11)$$

95

In general, the aggregate $\mathcal{F}(t)$ is composed of flows of different traffic types i for which the PMRRs K_i remain rather constant over time. For admission, each flow is supposed to register at the AC entity with its peak rate $r_{f_i^{new}}$ and its traffic type i. This yields type-specific reservations $R_i(t)$ for which $\sum_{i=0}^{n} R_i(t) = R(t)$ holds. On arrival of a new flow f_i^{new}, $R_i(t)$ is increased by the peak rate $r_{f_i^{new}}$ of the flow and it is decreased by the same bandwidth when the flow terminates. The value $\alpha_i(t) = \frac{R_i(t)}{R(t)}$ reflects the share of a traffic type i in the traffic mix. The entire traffic composition consisting of n different traffic types is then denoted by vector

$$\alpha(t) = \begin{pmatrix} \alpha_1(t) \\ \vdots \\ \alpha_n(t) \end{pmatrix}, \quad \sum_{i=1}^{n} \alpha_i(t) = 1. \tag{3.12}$$

EBAC with TSOB uses the information about the PMRRs K_i and the time-dependent traffic composition $\alpha(t)$ to estimate type-specific reservation utilizations $U_i(t)$. The estimation of the reservation utilizations $U_i(t)$ is a rather complex task and is described in Section 3.5.3. The values $U_i(t)$ are stored as hits in bins of separate histograms $P_i(t, U)$ which yield type-specific reservation utilization percentiles $U_{p,i}(t)$. We weight these percentiles by their corresponding shares $\alpha_i(t)$ and finally calculate the compound overbooking factor for EBAC with TSOB as

$$\varphi_c(t) = \frac{1}{\sum_i \alpha_i(t) \cdot U_{p,i}(t)}. \tag{3.13}$$

3.5.3 Estimation of Type-Specific Reservation Utilizations

A crucial issue for the performance of EBAC with TSOB is the estimation of type-specific reservation utilizations $U_i(t)$. Making type-specific measurements $M_i(t)$ yields exact values for $U_i(t) = \frac{M_i(t)}{R_i(t)}$. For a reduced number of traffic classes, type-specific measurements are feasible using current network technologies such as differentiated services (DiffServ) for traffic differentiation and multi protocol label switching (MPLS) for the collection of traffic statistics.

However, most routers do not provide type-specific traffic measurements and, therefore, the available parameters $M(t)$, $R(t)$, $R_i(t)$, and $\alpha(t)$ are used to estimate the values $U_i(t)$. In the following, two methods are developed to obtain estimates for the type-specific reservation utilizations.

Estimation with Linear Equation Systems (LES)

The first method tries to calculate the type-specific reservation utilizations $U_i(t)$ as solution of a linear program and uses the equation $U(t) = \sum_i \alpha_i(t) \cdot U_i(t)$ which leads to a linear equation system (LES) (cf. e.g. [123]) of the form

$$
\begin{pmatrix} U(t_{j-n}) \\ \vdots \\ U(t_j) \end{pmatrix} = \begin{pmatrix} \alpha_1(t_{j-n}) \dots \alpha_n(t_{j-n}) \\ \vdots \qquad \vdots \\ \alpha_1(t_j) \ \dots \ \alpha_n(t_j) \end{pmatrix} \begin{pmatrix} U_1(t_j) \\ \vdots \\ U_n(t_j) \end{pmatrix}, \qquad (3.14)
$$

where n is the number of traffic types and j denotes a time index. Let $\mathcal{U}(t_j)$ denote the left-hand vector, $\mathcal{A}(t_j)$ the central matrix, and $\mathcal{U}_i(t_j)$ the right-hand vector in Equation (3.14), then we have $\mathcal{U}(t_j) = \mathcal{A}(t_j) \cdot \mathcal{U}_i(t_j)$. Hence, a unique solution of the LES requires probes of $U(t)$ and $\alpha(t)$ for $t \in [t_{j-n}, t_j]$ and n linearly independent column vectors in $\mathcal{A}(t_j)$, i.e. $\det(\mathcal{A}(t_j)) \neq 0$. We calculate a new solution of the LES every time the vector $\alpha(t)$ changes significantly, i.e., $\exists k : \frac{|a_k(t_i) - a_k(t_{i-1})|}{a_k(t_i)} > \epsilon$. A problem of estimating type-specific reservation utilizations with the LES method is that the linear independence of the column vectors in $\mathcal{A}(t_j)$ is not guaranteed at any time t_j when the traffic composition changes. In this case, a unique solution for the equation system does not exist and the values $U_i(t_j)$ cannot be included in the histogram $P_i(t, U)$. Therefore, we simply insert the utilizations $U_i(t_{j-x})$ of the last feasible LES until a new linearly independent LES is found.

Algorithm 1 illustrates the computation of matrix $\mathcal{A}(t_j)$ with linearly independent column vectors. It takes the current traffic composition vector $\alpha(t_j)$, the previous matrix $\mathcal{A}(t_{j-1})$, and a set $\mathcal{L}$ of unused α-vectors as input parameters

---

Input: traffic composition vector $\alpha(t_j)$, previous matrix $\mathcal{A}(t_{j-1})$,
set $\mathcal{L}$ of unused vectors $\alpha(t)$

if $\mathcal{A}(t_{j-1}) = NULL$ **then**
   $\mathcal{A}(t_j) := \alpha(t_j)^T$ {first call}
   RETURN($\mathcal{A}(t_j)$)
else
   $\tilde{\alpha}(t_j) := \alpha(t_j)$
   if $\mathcal{L} \neq \emptyset$ **then**
      $\mathcal{L} := \mathcal{L} \cup \alpha(t_j)$
      $\tilde{\alpha}(t_j) := \text{BUILDEWMAVECTOR}(\mathcal{L})$
      NORMALIZE($\tilde{\alpha}(t_j)$)
   end if
   $\mathcal{A}(t_j) := \mathcal{A}(t_{j-1})$
   $n := \text{NUMBEROFELEMENTS}(\alpha(t_j))$
   if $\text{rank}(\mathcal{A}(t_j)) = n$ **then**
      REMOVEFIRSTCOLUMN($\mathcal{A}(t_j)$)
   end if
   APPENDLASTCOLUMN($\mathcal{A}(t_j), \tilde{\alpha}(t_j)^T$)
   if $\det(\mathcal{A}(t_j)) \neq 0$ **then**
      $\mathcal{L} := \emptyset$
      RETURN($\mathcal{A}(t_j)$)
   else
      RETURN($\mathcal{A}(t_{j-1})$)
   end if
end if

Output: matrix $\mathcal{A}(t_j)$

Algorithm 1: GENERATESHAREMATRIX: computation of linearly independent matrix column vectors.

and returns a linearly independent matrix $\mathcal{A}(t_j)$ with $1 \le i \le n$ columns.

The first call of this algorithm returns the transposed column vector $\alpha(t_i)$ as an $n \times 1$ matrix. For any further call, vector $\tilde{\alpha}(t_j)$ is initialized with $\alpha(t_j)$. If there are recent α-vectors not yet considered in $\mathcal{A}(t_{j-1})$, i.e. $\mathcal{L} \neq \emptyset$, then $\alpha(t_j)$ joins $\mathcal{L}$ and $\tilde{\alpha}(t_j)$ is set as an exponentially-weighted moving average (EWMA) [116] of all yet unconsidered α-vectors in $\mathcal{L}$. The EWMA is calculated over vector elements α_i such that

$$\tilde{\alpha}_i(t_x) = \begin{cases} \alpha_i(t_{min}) & \text{if } t_{min} \text{ is earliest time index in } \mathcal{L} \\ \beta \cdot \tilde{\alpha}_i(t_{x-1}) + (1-\beta) \cdot \alpha_i(t_x) & \text{else.} \end{cases}$$

(3.15)

In Equation (3.15), the devaluation parameter $\beta \in [0, 1]$ controls the influence of older values $\tilde{\alpha}_i(t_x)$ whose impact decays exponentially with β. The computation of $\tilde{\alpha}(t_j) = (\tilde{\alpha}_1(t_j), \ldots, \tilde{\alpha}_n(t_j))$ can lead to $\sum_{i=1}^{n} \tilde{\alpha}_i(t_j) \neq 1$ and, therefore, vector $\tilde{\alpha}(t_j)$ must be normalized after the application of the EWMA algorithm.

Finally, we construct a new matrix $\mathcal{A}(t_j)$ from the matrix $\mathcal{A}(t_{j-1})$ by removing the oldest α-vector from $\mathcal{A}(t_{j-1})$ and appending the transposed vector $\tilde{\alpha}(t_j)$ to it. However, if the input matrix $\mathcal{A}(t_{j-1})$ is not of size $n \times n$, a column is appended but none is removed. The constructed matrix $\mathcal{A}(t_j)$ is then tested for linear independency and, if $\det(A) \neq 0$, it is returned by the algorithm which also empties the set $\mathcal{L}$ of unconsidered α-vectors. Otherwise, the previous matrix $\mathcal{A}(t_{j-1})$ is returned.

Algorithm 1 requires at least n calls before it can provide a matrix with linearly independent column vectors as necessary for a unique solution of Equation (3.14). Since linear independency cannot be guaranteed for each new vector $\alpha(t)$, the successive computation of type-specific reservation utilizations by the LES method is potentially fragmentary. Therefore, this method must be considered as approximation of the type-specific reservation utilizations $U_i(t)$.

Estimation with Least Squares Approximation (LSA)

The second approach estimates the type-specific reservation utilizations $U_i(t)$ using a least squares approximation (LSA, cf. e.g. [124]). For the ease of understanding, we illustrate this method, without loss of generality, for two different traffic types $i \in \{1, 2\}$. The variables $U_1(t)$ and $U_2(t)$ denote their type-specific reservation utilizations. The global reservation utilization is calculated as $U(t) = \alpha_1(t) \cdot U_1(t) + \alpha_2(t) \cdot U_2(t)$ and with $\alpha_1(t) + \alpha_2(t) = 1$ we get

$$U(t) = \alpha_1(t) \cdot (U_1(t) - U_2(t)) + U_2(t). \qquad (3.16)$$

We substitute $a_j = U_1(t_j) - U_2(t_j)$ and $b_j = U_2(t_j)$ and obtain the least squares error ε for parameters $U_1(t)$ and $U_2(t)$ if we minimize the term

$$\varepsilon = \min_{a_m, b_m} \sum_{j=1}^{m} [U(t_j) - (\alpha_1(t_j) \cdot a_m + b_m)]^2. \qquad (3.17)$$

The time index j thereby covers all values $U(t_j)$ and $\alpha(t_j)$ from the first probe ($j = 1$) to the last ($j = m$) probe ever determined by the EBAC system. We find the minimum of ε where the first derivatives of Equation (3.17) yield zero, i.e., we set $\frac{\partial \varepsilon}{\partial a} \overset{!}{=} 0$ und $\frac{\partial \varepsilon}{\partial b} \overset{!}{=} 0$ and resolve these equations to parameters a_m and b_m which yields

$$a_m = \frac{m \cdot \sum_j \alpha_1(t_j) U(t_j) - \sum_j \alpha_1(t_j) \cdot \sum_j U(t_j)}{m \cdot \sum_j \alpha_1(t_j)^2 - \left(\sum_j \alpha_1(t_j)\right)^2} \qquad (3.18)$$

$$b_m = \frac{\sum_j U(t_j) \cdot \sum_j \alpha_1(t_j)^2 - \sum_j \alpha_1(t_j) \cdot \sum_j \alpha_1(t_j) U(t_j)}{m \cdot \sum_j \alpha_1(t_j)^2 - \left(\sum_j \alpha_1(t_j)\right)^2} \qquad (3.19)$$

for $1 \leq j \leq m$. The sums in Equations (3.18) and (3.19) can be computed iteratively which helps to cope with the large set of parameter values observed over all times t_j. In addition, we apply the TEWMA algorithm to these sums to blind out short-time fluctuations. Let $\mathcal{S}_m$ denote any of the sums in Equations (3.18) and (3.19) at time t_m, then the TEWMA at time t_{m+1} is

$$\mathcal{S}(t_{m+1}) = \mathcal{S}(t_m) \cdot e^{-\gamma \cdot (t_{m+1} - t_m)} + x(t_{m+1}), \qquad (3.20)$$

where $x(t_{m+1})$ denotes the addend at time t_{m+1} of the respective sum. In Equation (3.20), the devaluation factor $\gamma \in [0, 1]$ leads to an exponential decay of old values $x(t_j)_{j \leq m}$ in the sum $\mathcal{S}$. This incremental implementation of the LSA method is efficient and enables its application to more than two different traffic types. With the calculated parameters a_m and b_m, the estimates for the type-specific reservation utilizations are finally obtained as $U_1(t_m) = a_m + b_m$ and $U_2(t_m) = b_m$.

Comparison of Measured and Estimated Type-Specific Reservation Utilizations

We perform simulations with both methods approximating the type-specific reservation utilizations as described in the previous two sections. For the sake of clarity, we simulate with only two different traffic types $i \in \{1, 2\}$. Type 1 has a mean PMRR of $E[K_1] = 2$ and an initial mean share of $E[\alpha_1] = 0.2$ in the traffic mix. Traffic type 2 is characterized by $E[K_2] = 8$ and $E[\alpha_2] = 0.8$. Both simulations use the same seed for the random number generator to exclude effects of different statistical characteristics of the simulated traffic. This guarantees a fair comparison of the results.

Figure 3.20(a) shows a comparison of the measured type-specific reservation utilizations $U_i^M(t)$ and their corresponding estimates $U_i^{LES}(t)$ obtained by the LES method. Figure 3.20(b) compares the values $U_i^M(t)$ to their approximations $U_i^{LSA}(t)$ achieved with the LSA method. The measured and the type-specific reservation utilizations are determined every second.

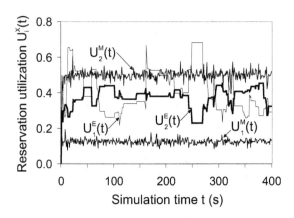

(a) Estimation with linear equation systems.

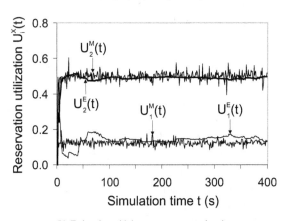

(b) Estimation with least squares approximation.

Figure 3.20: *Comparison of measured and estimated type-specific reservation utilizations.*

On the packet level, we have Poisson distributed inter-arrival times which lead to short-time fluctuations for the measured values $U_i^M(t)$. These fluctuations are clearly damped by the TEWMA algorithm used for the estimated values $U_i^{LES}(t)$ and $U_i^{LSA}(t)$. Obviuosly, the LES method is not feasible for the approximation of type-specific reservation utilizations since the resulting estimates deviate strongly from the exact measurements. In contrast, the LSA method provides good estimates for the corresponding measured utilizations. Hence, this approach enables EBAC with TSOB without type-specific traffic measurements.

3.5.4 Performance Comparison of Conventional EBAC and EBAC with TSOB

To investigate EBAC with TSOB, we perform multiple simulations each associated with a different traffic situation. For all simulations, we use a link capacity $c_l = 10$ Mbit/s and simulate with two traffic types $i \in \{1, 2\}$ with mean PMRRs $E[K_1] = 2$ and $E[K_2] = 8$. Flows f of any type reserve bandwidth with a peak rate $r_f = 768$ Kbit/s. This guarantees fair flow blocking probabilities $p_b(t)$ on link l which is always saturated with flow requests. For conventional EBAC, the overbooking factor $\varphi(t)$ is calculated according to Equation (3.5). For EBAC with TSOB, the compound overbooking factor $\varphi_c(t)$ is computed as defined in Equation (3.13). The reservation utilization percentile parameter is set to $p_u = 0.95$. We investigate EBAC with TSOB for a static traffic mix before we study its behavior for sudden changes of the traffic composition $\alpha(t)$.

Simulation with Constant Traffic Mix

This first experiment simulates traffic with static mean shares $E[\alpha_i]$, i.e., the composition of the traffic mix remains constant except for statistical fluctuations. The results of a single simulation run are shown in Figure 3.21(a) for conventional EBAC and in Figure 3.21(b) for EBAC with TSOB. The initial mean shares of the traffic types in the mix are set to $E[\alpha_1] = 0.2$ and $E[\alpha_2] = 0.8$.

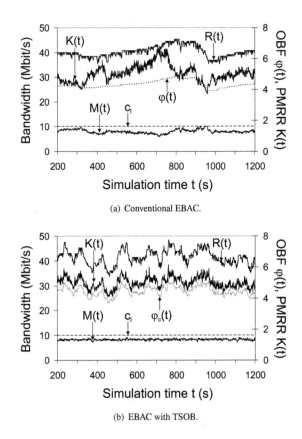

(a) Conventional EBAC.

(b) EBAC with TSOB.

Figure 3.21: *Adaptation of overbooking factor with conventional EBAC and EBAC with TSOB for a constant traffic mix.*

EBAC	$E[U_l]$	$c_{var}[U_l]$	$E[p_d]$
CONV	0.8231	0.0908	$6.57 \cdot 10^{-6}$
TSOB	0.8518	0.0396	0

Table 3.7: *Link utilization and packet delay probability of conventional EBAC (CONV) and EBAC with type-specific overbooking (TSOB) for a constant traffic mix.*

For conventional EBAC (cf. Figure 3.21(a)), the overbooking factor $\varphi(t)$ adapts rather slowly to changes of the traffic mix that are due to statistical fluctuations of $\alpha(t)$. Therefore, the link capacity may be under- or overutilized and, in the latter case, the QoS may be at risk. In contrast, EBAC with TSOB (cf. Figure 3.21(b)) adjusts its compound overbooking factor $\varphi_c(t)$ very quickly to the variations of $\alpha(t)$. Decreases of the aggregate PMRR $K(t)$ due to statistical fluctuations of $\alpha(t)$ lead to a significant decreases of $\varphi_c(t)$ and increases of $K(t)$ cause significant increases of $\varphi_c(t)$. As a consequence, EBAC with TSOB keeps the measured rate $M(t)$ on a higher and more stable level than conventional EBAC. This, in turn, leads to an increased and even link utilization and also supports the compliance with QoS guarantees. The illustration of a single simulation run shows clearly the better responsiveness of EBAC with TSOB compared to that of conventional EBAC. Table 3.7 compares the mean $E[U_l]$ and the coefficient of variation $c_{var}[U_l]$ of the link utilization U_l for conventional EBAC and EBAC with TSOB. The values are averages over the entire simulation time. The results show that EBAC with TSOB increases and stabilizes U_l and, in addition, reduces the mean packet delay probability $E[p_d]$.

Simulation with Changing Traffic Mix

The following two simulation experiments focus on the behavior of EBAC with TSOB after a decrease or increase of the traffic intensity due to changes of the traffix mix $\alpha(t)$. We consider sudden changes of $\alpha(t)$ to have worst case scenarios and to obtain upper bounds on the EBAC response times.

EBAC	$E[U_l]$	$c_{var}[U_l]$	$E[p_d]$
CONV	0.7594	0.1972	$1.57 \cdot 10^{-4}$
TSOB	0.8243	0.0416	0

Table 3.8: *Link utilization and packet delay probability of conventional EBAC (CONV) and EBAC with type-specific overbooking (TSOB) for decreasing traffic intensity.*

Simulation with Decreasing Traffic Intensity We investigate a change of the traffic intensity from a high to a low value. Figures 3.22(a) and 3.22(b) show the average results over 50 simulation runs. We use the same two traffic types with their characteristic PMRRs as before. However, we start with mean traffic shares $E[\alpha_1] = 0.8$ and $E[\alpha_2] = 0.2$. At simulation time $t_0 = 1000$ s, the type-specific request arrival rates λ_{f_i} are changed such that the mean shares of both traffic types are swapped to $E[\alpha_1] = 0.2$ and $E[\alpha_2] = 0.8$. Hence, the traffic intensity of the entire aggregate decreases due to a change in the traffic mix $\alpha(t)$. The corresponding sudden increase of the aggregate PMRR $K(t)$ results in an immediate decrease of the measured traffic $M(t)$ for conventional EBAC (cf. Figure 3.22(a)). With observable delay, the conventional overbooking factor $\varphi(t)$ is adapted as a result of the slowly decreasing p_u-percentile $U_p(t)$ obtained from the histogram $P(t, U)$. From the simulation results in Section 3.4.2 we know that this delay strongly depends on the EBAC memory defined by the half-life period T_H in Equation (3.6). In contrast, EBAC with TSOB (cf. Figure 3.22(b)) increases its overbooking factor $\varphi_c(t)$ promptly since the percentiles $U_{p,i}(t)$ of the type-specific histograms $P_i(t, U)$ remain rather constant. Only the shares of the traffic types in the traffic mix change and, therefore, $\varphi_c(t)$ is immediately adapted. Compared to conventional EBAC, the faster reaction of EBAC with TSOB leads to a higher and more stable link utilization and also reduces the packet delay probability as shown in Table 3.8. The shown numbers are mean values over the 50 simulation runs.

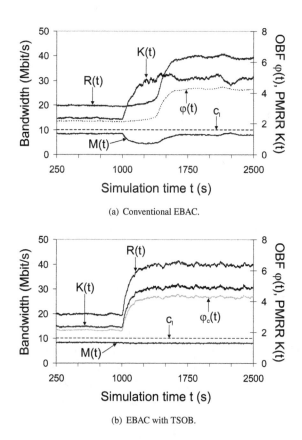

(a) Conventional EBAC.

(b) EBAC with TSOB.

Figure 3.22: *Adaptation of overbooking factor with conventional EBAC and EBAC with TSOB for decreasing traffic intensity.*

EBAC	$E[U_l]$	$c_{var}[U_l]$	$E[p_d]$
CONV	0.8515	0.0868	$8.03 \cdot 10^{-3}$
TSOB	0.8329	0.0399	0

Table 3.9: *Link utilization and packet delay probability of conventional EBAC (CONV) and EBAC with type-specific overbooking (TSOB) for increasing traffic intensity.*

Simulation with Increasing Traffic Intensity   We now change the traffic intensity from a low to a high level which leads to a decrease of the aggregate PMRR $K(t)$. The simulation results are shown in Figures 3.23(a) and 3.23(b). Using the same two traffic types as before, we start with mean traffic shares $E[\alpha_1] = 0.2$ and $E[\alpha_2] = 0.8$ and swap them at simulation time $t_0 = 1000$ s to $E[\alpha_1] = 0.8$ and $E[\alpha_2] = 0.2$ by changing the type-specific request arrival rates λ_{f_i}. This change in the traffic mix $\alpha(t)$ increases the traffic intensity of the admitted aggregate. In this experiment, the QoS is at risk because flows with low traffic intensity are successively replaced by flows with high intensity and, therefore, the load on the link is rising. Like for decreasing traffic intensity, conventional EBAC (cf. Figure 3.22(a)) reacts slower than EBAC with TSOB (cf. Figure 3.22(b)) although this time, their speed of adapting their respective overbooking factors $\varphi(t)$ and $\varphi_c(t)$ differs less. From the simulation results in Section 3.4.3 we know that the QoS restoration time T_R^Q of conventional EBAC is independent of the EBAC memory in case of a sudden traffic increase. Our simluation results compiled in Table 3.9 show that conventional EBAC yields a slightly higher link utilization compared to EBAC with TSOB. However, this high utilization comes at the expense of a violation of QoS guarantees as the measured traffic $M(t)$ consumes the entire link capacity c_l for a short period of time (cf. Figure 3.22(a)). As shown in Table 3.9, the mean packet delay probability $E[p_d]$ is rising significantly. This exposure to loss of QoS guarantees obviously favours the extension of EBAC towards TSOB since it immediately detects changes in the composition of the traffic mix and thus stabilizes the link utilization as indicated by $c_{var}[U_l]$.

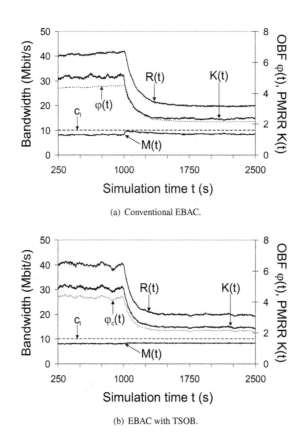

(a) Conventional EBAC.

(b) EBAC with TSOB.

Figure 3.23: *Adaptation of overbooking factor with conventional EBAC and EBAC with TSOB for increasing traffic intensity.*

Summary

We have illustrated the extension of EBAC towards type-specific overbooking (TSOB). A compound overbooking factor $\varphi_c(t)$ is calculated based on the type-specific reservation utilizations $U_i(t)$. In general, the values $U_i(t)$ cannot be measured directly and, therefore, we estimate them by the application of either a linear equation system (LES) or a least squares approximation (LSA). Our simulation results show that only the LSA method is able to derive the estimates for $U_i(t)$ with sufficiently high accuracy. EBAC with TSOB increases the link utilization for stationary traffic mixes as more traffic can be savely admitted with this system extension. For variable traffic mixes, sudden changes of the traffic intensity are simulated by decreasing or increasing the share of flows with highly utilized reservations. If the share of these flows, i.e. the traffic intensity, decreases, EBAC with TSOB reacts faster than conventional EBAC which leads to a higher and more stable link utilization during the adaptation of the overbooking factor. If the share of these flows increases, the advantage of EBAC with TSOB over conventional EBAC becomes even more obvious. While EBAC with TSOB can avoid overload situations for an increase of the traffic intensity due to changes in the traffic mix, conventional EBAC has no appropriate means to prevent such situations.

3.6 EBAC in a Network Scope

The performance of experience-based admission control (EBAC) has intensively been studied by simulations on a single link. A simple deployment of EBAC in an entire network is the link-by-link application of the concept. However, this method requires a lot of signaling which may lead to scalability problems. Another possibility performs AC only at the network border by using separate instances of EBAC at all network ingress routers. This approach guarantees scalability but requires further investigation of the resulting distributed network admission control (NAC) system.

A prototype applying EBAC at the network border exists for the purely IP-based network architecture of the KING (Key components for the Internet of the Next Generation) project [125, 126]. Its implementation requires the survey, synchronization, and correlation of many distributed network information about, e.g. resource reservations of flows admitted at the ingress routers, traffic measurements on the links, routing and load balancing in the network. As a consequence, the network-wide admission decisions cannot be made independently of each other since they have a correlated impact on the link loads in the network.

However, if a network architecture fulfills certain requirements, the application of EBAC in the scope of an entire network is well feasible. The border-to-border (b2b) budget-based network admission control (BBB-NAC) is one of four approaches presented in Section 3.1.3 (cf. Figure 3.1(c)). The BBB-NAC implements admission control (AC) at the border of a network and uses directed b2b tunnels with pre-determined capacities. In a simple network-scoped implementation, these tunnel capacities can be overbooked by EBAC like physical link capacities, i.e., the tunnels are considered as virtual links. This approach requires separate EBAC instances for all capacity tunnels and, hence, the complexity of the problem is now reduced to appropriate tunnel dimensioning and to b2b aggregate-specific traffic measurements. If the network is based on, for instance, the (generalized) multi-protocol label switching ((G)MPLS) architecture [31,38], tunnels can be implemented as label switched paths (LSPs) between border routers and

111

traffic can be easily measured per tunnel. Label distribution protocol (LDP) traffic matrices [127] provide the necessary information for the established LSPs.

In the next chapter, we will show how the tunnel sizes can be calculated depending on certain network characteristics such as routing, traffic matrix, and flow blocking probabilities.

4 Adaptive Bandwidth Allocation (ABA)

In this chapter, we give an overview of existing technologies for the management of network resources in transport networks and consider adaptive bandwidth allocation (ABA) for capacity tunnels that can be used to save bandwidth in such networks. Virtual tunnels connecting two border routers in a transport network are a popular means for traffic engineering (TE). They can be used for route pinning as well as for admission control purposes and, hence, for control of the network traffic. Applying ABA to these TE tunnels allows for bandwidth savings and reduces the capital expenditures (CAPEX) of internet service providers (ISPs) for their network infrastructures. ISPs are facing two major challenges today: the permanent increase of traffic and the common request for Quality of Service (QoS). To master the first issue and to guarantee the second, ISPs must control the congestion level in their networks. This can be achieved by means of TE which also includes the management of network resources. In recent years, a lot of new networking technologies have emerged for a variety of transmission media such as air, copper line, and optical fiber. Each technology is subject to the limited amount of available network resources and, therefore, requires its own special resource management. At first, we give a general overview of network resource management (NRM), locate the placement of NRM in the network landscape, and point out the necessity of NRM for QoS in the Internet. We present the most common architectures, protocols, and technologies for the implementation of network resource management and focus on bandwidth allocation as a central instance of many problems related to NRM. The main part of this chapter concerns ABA for capacity tunnels. We first describe the considered resource allocation problem and then investigate the performance of ABA with regard to different influence parameters. We thereby show the impact of different traffic demand models and tunnel implementations on the bandwidths savings achievable with ABA for capacity tunnels. In addition, the impact of resilience requirements on theses savings is briefly discussed.

4.1 Overview of Network Resource Management (NRM)

This section considers network resource management (NRM) in general, locates the application area of NRM in the network landscape, shows its necessity for QoS provisioning, and classifies existing NRM architectures, protocols, and technologies. Finally, bandwidth allocation is identified as a central problem of NRM.

4.1.1 NRM in the Network Landscape

The logical structure of todays transport networks is traditionally divided into three sections known as data, control, and management plane [64]. Each plane has its own functions that operate on plane-specific states describing facets of the current network condition. These states depend on each other and, therefore, mutual information exchange between the different planes is required (cf. Figure 4.1). The major tasks of the individual network planes are the following:

- **Data plane** The data plane is also called forwarding or transport plane. Its primary task is to forward traffic, thus delivering data to its destination. Forwarding information bases (FIBs) such as IP routing tables [1] or MPLS label information bases [31] are used to make forwarding decisions. The forwarding task is performed as fast as possible (ideally in light

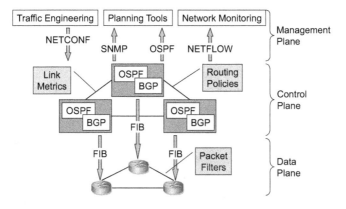

Figure 4.1: *Logical division of a network in functional planes.*

speed) and, therefore, its implementations are all hardware-based and increasingly shifted to the optical domain. Other tasks of this plane are the filtering and the queueing of packets. The functional components of the data plane operate on very small time scales in the order of micro- to milli-seconds.

- **Control plane** The control plane has the ability to route network traffic. Its tasks cover everything that directly controls the data plane, e.g. routing, protection and restoration, signaling, resource reservation, admission control, flow classification, and many others. To accomplish all these task, the control plane runs different protocols like the open shortest path first (OSPF) protocol [25] and the border gateway protocol (BGP) [27] for intra- and inter-domain routing. In general, these protocols run autonomously, distribute relevant information, e.g. link metrics and routing policies, within the network, and also provide such information to the management plane. The functional components of the control plane operate on larger time scales in the order of milli-seconds to seconds.

- **Management plane** The managment plane manages the overall technical infrastructure of the network, i.e., it coordinates functions among all
three planes. To reach that goal, it receives network information from the
control and the data plane and, in turn, controls these planes by the configuration of network devices. Some tasks of the management plane are close
to the infrastructure such as network monitoring and also fault, policy, and
security management. Some other tasks considering network planning or
traffic engineering are located on a higher level. Examples for protocols
processed on the management plane are the simple network management
protocol (SNMP), NETFLOW, NETCONF, and many different proprietary command line interface (CLI) protocols. These protocols are used
for information retrieval and network configuration. The functional components of the management plane operate on relatively large time scales
in the order of seconds to days.

The three network planes make NRM a distributed problem. The management plane is used for making management policy decisions and is controlled
by human beings. The control plane enforces the management policies through
automatic processes that configure the network devices. The data plane implements the management policies by rules of traffic forwarding. The interoperation
between the three planes and the heterogeneity of networking technologies and
corresponding devices induce a lot of complexity to the network management. As
a consequence, some effort is made to reduce this complexity. For instance, the
common control and measurement plane (CCAMP) working group of the internet engineering task force (IETF) aims at "... *defining a common control plane
and a separate common measurement plane for physical path and core tunneling
technologies of Internet and telecom service providers* ... " [39]. For that purpose, the generalized multi-protocol label switching (GMPLS) framework [38]
has been developed. However, the GMPLS framework is mainly focused on the
standardization of protocols for a unified control plane.

4.1.2 Necessity of NRM

In the early years of the Internet, the management of network resources was not a big issue. The offered services were simple and the corresponding transmitted data volume was limited. Reachability and connectivity of communication end points were of major interest and emphasized the aspect of survivable network. With the increasing number of QoS-sensitive services (VoIP, VoD, IPTV) and the increasing volume of corresponding data traffic, ISPs face a great challenge today. They have to map steadily increasing traffic demands to the limited transmission resources available in their networks. The transition from best effort to QoS services with guaranteed performances in terms of blocking, loss, and delay of traffic makes NRM a very important issue. This does not only hold for transport networks [64, 128] but for all kinds of communication networks such as, e.g., mobile communication networks [129], wireless local area (WLAN) networks [130], and satellite networks [131], using many different types of transmission resources [76].

The enforcement of QoS constraints requires the allocation of network resources dedicated to high-quality communication services [45]. In general, requested network resources are expressed by bandwidth demands that bind a fraction of the transmission capacity of the network if granted. Depending on the network type, these capacities are either hard (e.g. in WDM networks) or soft (e.g. in UMTS networks) and, therefore, require different implementations of NRM. However, all implementations of NRM have the same objective, i.e., they aim at the efficient use of network resources and, simultaneously, at the protection against overutilization of these resources.

4.1.3 Network Technologies, Protocols, and Architectures with Impact on NRM

Network resource management in traditional public switched telephone networks (PSTNs) is rather simple. The resources consumed by a single communication

channel are standardized and unified, e.g. 64 Kbit/s for a single integrated services digital network (ISDN) channel. The signaling on the control plane of
PSTNs has been standardized in the 1980s by the *Comité Consultatif International Télégraphique et Téléphonique* (CCITT), now known as the *International
Telecommunication Union* (ITU). The de facto standard is the Signaling System 7 (SS7) [132] that takes care of call control, transaction control, and other
applications. Due to the connection-oriented switching and the physically constrained switching capabilities of the hardware, the number of simultaneous calls
is limited in a PSTN. In case of overload, further call attempts are simply blocked
and, therefore, the QoS of already established connections can always be guaranteed.

Network resource management in connectionless, i.e. packet-based, communication networks is more complex due to the heterogeneity of networking technologies and their associated tranmsmission resources [133]. We disregard the
problems and solutions existing for wireless networks and focus on the dominating technologies in the scope of transport networks. The most important current
and future networking technologies, protocols, and architectures for NRM are
presented. A general overview of NRM issues for the emerging Internet QoS can
be found in [134].

Transmission Control Protocol and Internet Protocol

The transmission control protocol (TCP) [4] and the Internet protocol version 4
(IPv4) [1] and version 6 (IPv6) [135] represent the de facto standard protocols on
the transport and the network layer of the Internet. Although these protocols are
not intended to be used for NRM, they have a considerable impact on it.

Transmission Control Protocol (TCP)   The majority of traffic present
in the Internet today is comprised of TCP flows. Standard TCP does not provide
any mechanism for controlling the bandwidth allocated to a particular TCP flow.
However, the flow control mechanism inherent to TCP implicitly implements a

bandwidth sharing concept. Two TCP connections which have the same round-trip time (RTT) generally receive an equal share of the bandwidth at a particular bottleneck link (cf. e.g. [17], pp. 256). Equal bandwidth sharing is desirable if the connections belong to different users of a network. A single user certainly wants to prioritize different applications and distribute bandwidth according to his or her own preferences. This is certainly the case when multiple TCP connections with different RTT coexist, because TCP favors short RTT connections which can receive a much larger share of bandwidth at a bottleneck link than flows with larger RTT [136]. To control the bandwidth consumption of concurrent TCP flows, bandwidth sharing mechanisms like, e.g., weighted fair queuing [52] have been investigated. Similar mechanisms can also be used to improve the applicability of TCP with respect to service differentiation [137].

Internet Protocol (IP)   IP is the glue that keeps the Internet together. Routing protocols like OSPF and BGP use IP address information to set up routing tables based on which all Internet traffic is forwarded to its destination. Connectivity and reachability is the primary task of IP which has no explicit resource management capabilities. However, the routing according to the rules of IP has a serious impact on the consumption of network resources. Traffic within an Autonomous System (AS) is mostly routed on shortest paths. The length of a path is determined by a routing protocol dependent link metric. The setting of these metrics decides on the ways taken by the traffic and also on the consumed network resources. According to shortest path principle, all flows traversing two different routers in the same order are routed on the same path between these routers. This can lead to overloaded and poorly utilized links at the same time. Traffic that requires real-time transportation needs paths on which enough resources are available, but the IP routing mechanism is generally unaware of free link capacities. The IP routing constraint together with the setting of link metrics makes IP routing within ASs a very difficult optimization problem [138, 139] and, therefore, IP is not a suitable means for an overall NRM solution.

Synchronous Optical Network (SONET) and Synchronous Digital Hierarchy (SDH)

The technologies of Synchronous Optical Network (SONET) [140] and Synchronous Digital Hierarchy (SDH) [141] have emerged in the 1980s and replaced the Plesiochronous Digital Hierarchy (PDH) technique in asynchronous networks. Today, they represent the de facto standards for the frame-based transport of data on the link layer of optical and electronical high-speed networks [142]. SONET was developed in North America by an American National Standards Institute (ANSI) accredited committee whereas SDH was developed in parallel by the CCITT in Europe. Due to the world-wide cooperation between the standards organizations, SONET and SDH equipment is now widely compatible, a fact that facilitates operations, administration, and maintenance (OA&M) of today's transport networks. A good introduction to SONET and SDH standards can be found in [64].

The primary task of SONET/SDH is the point-to-point-oriented transport of aggregated data. To reach that goal, the problem of traffic grooming [143] must be solved. An optimal solution to that problem improves the network throughput and reduces the number of add/drop multiplexers (ADMs) and thus the cost of network infrastructure. Another major task of SONET/SDH technology is fast protection switching which increases the service availability and network survivability through redundancy provisioning [144]. Self-healing SONET/SDH rings [145] represent a very common architecture for metropolitan area networks (MANs). In wide area networks (WANs), SONET/SDH path selection and protection mechanisms [146] solve the problem of finding disjoint paths (cf. e.g. [147]) and thus contribute to the network fault tolerance. Considering the point-to-point oriented scope of SONET/SDH, this technology is intended for protected data transport and does not provide the necessary means for net-wide NRM.

Wavelength Division Multiplex (WDM)

The transition to optical wavelength division multiplex (WDM) systems [148] has been driven by increasing demands for communication bandwidth. Initially intended to enlarge the capacity of point-to-point communication on the already-installed fiber plant, it is now increasingly deployed for optical ring and mesh networks. Industry standards for WDM systems have been developed under the leadership of the ITU. A good overview of the WDM technology is given, for instance, in [149].

Research and development of optical WDM networks have matured considerably in the recent years. The currently most promising approach to operate WDM networks is to use optical transmission in combination with electronical circuit switching which equals a concatenation of wavelengths resulting in a network path. Such a path is also called a lightpath that spans multiple fiber links with wavelength bypass facilities in the network nodes. The number of lightpaths in a network is limited due to the restricted number of wavelengths per fiber and the high cost of expensive wavelength transceivers. From this limitation originates a challenging networking problem called the routing and wavelength assignment (RWA) problem which is well known from literature (cf. e.g. [150]). The number of feasible lightpaths can be further increased through efficient wavelength conversion [151] in the network, i.e., lightpaths do not necessarily have identical wavelengths on every fiber. More research on WDM networks is dedicated to traffic grooming [143] and to protection and restoration [152]. Even though WDM provides the wavelength as a new dimension to be used for routing purposes, its main strength is the provisioning of large tranmission capacities. Therefore, an overall NRM solution on the optical WDM layer is not an option regarding its course resource granularity with wavelengths as smallest units.

Integrated Services (IntServ) Architecture

The IETF proposed the integrated services (IntServ) architecture [33] to enable services with guaranteed QoS [83] in the Internet. To reach that goal,

121

IntServ reserves network resources for each individual QoS-enabled traffic flow. A good overview of IntServ is given in [153]. The resource reservation protocol (RSVP) [16, 32] is used to establish reservations along the path of a flow. The routers along this path store the reservation information as states in their management information bases (MIBs). A reservation state contains a traffic specification of the flow and thereby indicates its expected bandwidth consumption. This information is used to manage the capacities of outgoing interfaces and to enforce policing and shaping of traffic on a per flow basis. Admission control (AC) mechanisms also use it to decide whether additional flows can be admitted to a path or not. With IntServ, the queuing and scheduling of individual flows becomes difficult if the number of simultaneously active flows is very large. Especially in the case of failing paths, i.e., when reservations have to be rebooked on other paths, the IntServ approach does not scale. To handle this problem, the IETF proposed the aggregation of RSVP-based reservations for IPv4 and IPv6 traffic in [154]. This measure improves the scalability of IntServ to some degree. However, the IntServ concept still lacks scalability and it can thus cnot be applied for NRM purposes in large-scale transport networks.

Differentiated Services (DiffServ) Architecture

To overcome the scalability problems of IntServ, the IETF proposed the differentiated services (DiffServ) architecture [48] which supports controlled load services [85] for the Internet. In contrast to IntServ, DiffServ does not consider individual traffic flows but differentiates the Internet traffic in only a few service classes receiving different QoS. Hence, the forwarding process operates on aggregated traffic. The DiffServ code point (DSCP) as part of the IP header identifies a service class and controls the per hop behavior (PHB) of IP packets in a router, i.e., the DSCP indicates whether a packet is treated with high or low priority in the forwarding process. As no per flow information is processed, the DiffServ architecture scales well for large networks. DiffServ relies on traffic policers and shapers at the network edges that control the traffic entering the network. However, this simple traffic conditioning impairs the QoS of all flows with equal DSCP. The original DiffServ approach lacks AC and thus does not support high QoS for some flows at the expense of rejecting other ones. Bandwidth brokers solve this problem by introducing AC on a per flow basis at the network edges. They account for the bandwidth consumption and the paths of all flows admitted to the network to avoid congestion on the links. Centralized bandwidth brokers face similar scalability issues [155] like IntServ. Therefore, distributed bandwidth broker architectures (cf. e.g. [156]) try to improve the scalability of the DiffServ AC. The corresponding AC design matches the ingress budget-based network admission control (IB NAC) described in Section 3.1.3. The investigation of the IB NAC in [63] reveals its poor performance regarding the resource utilization for a reasonable QoS level. Due to its resource inefficiency, the DiffServ architecture is inappropriate for an NRM in large-scale transport networks, too.

Multi-Protocol Label Switching (MPLS) and Generalized MPLS (GMPLS)

Some fundamentals of multi-protocol label switching (MPLS) and generalized MPLS (GMPLS) have already been described in Section 2.2.1. This section merely addresses further issues on resource management in connection with these two technologies.

The MPLS technology is a widely deployed network mechanism that offers various means for traffic engineering (TE). An IETF working group has specified the MPLS architecture [31]. Many further RFCs [157] standardize the application of MPLS to packet-oriented networks. MPLS is supported by all major manufacturers for network equipment like, e.g. Cisco, Juniper, Alcatel, and Huawei, who implement it in their router software. A practical introduction to MPLS and its particular application to network management in Cisco routers is given in [158]. The role of MPLS in the Internet is described in [159]. Many features for OA&M [160] qualify MPLS as a key technology for TE [34–36]

123

and NRM [161, 162] in today's IP networks. Packet flows transported through a MPLS network can be aggregated in forwarding equivalent classes (FECs). Packets belonging to the same FEC get the same forwarding treatment in the LSRs. Hence, FECs can be used to implement traffic and service class differentiation [163]. In addition, label stacking allows for the construction of label switched path (LSP) hierarchies [37], i.e., multiple lower-order LSPs can be nested in a higher-order LSP that is associated with a new label on top of the MPLS label stack. Together, FECs and LSP hierarchies make MPLS scalable. The MPLS signaling protocols RSVP-TE [29] and CR-LDP [30] can be used to set up LSPs along explicit routes that are computed by, e.g., a constrained shortest path first (CSPF) algorithm. Those LSP can be associated with a bandwidth that can be modified using the reservation control primitives of RSVP-TE or CR-LDP. A CSPF algorithm finds shortest feasible paths that may differ from those found by OSPF, but that fulfill certain QoS requirements for new LSPs with regard to parameters like bandwidth, delay, or the course of a LSP. As a consequence, explicit routing with CSPF improves the resource utilization in MPLS networks and controls where traffic is directed. MPLS also provides fast restoration techniques and the necessary protocol extensions [47] which automatically reroute LSPs in case of link or router failures to maintain QoS.

Generalized multi-protocol label switching (GMPLS) extends MPLS for application to optical networks. Hence, GMPLS is intended to be a technology-spanning mechanism for TE and NRM in heterogeneous network environments. The heterogeneity of supported networks induces much complexity to the implementation of NRM since multi-granular network resources such as, e.g., arbitrary low-order LSP bandwidths, TDM channel sizes, and wavelength capacities must be considered. Currently, much effort is dedicated to GMPLS standardization [39] as well as to research in GMPLS. The research topics primarily concern problems emerging from the integration of IP, MPLS, SONET/SDH, and WDM networks. One example is the routing and wavelength assignment (RWA) problem in the GMPLS hierarchy [164]. Due to the importance for QoS in the Internet, resilience and fault management [165, 166] in GMPLS-controlled networks is another issue for investigation. GMPLS is a promising approach towards a unified, standardized, and commonly accepted base for NRM. However, GMPLS solutions for any of the above problems require an efficient resource and bandwidth management [167, 168] to which we try to contribute with our approach for adaptive bandwidth tunnels as descibed in Section 4.2.

4.1.4 Bandwidth Allocation and Related Problems

Bandwidth allocation [169–172] (BA) is the reservation of transmission resources for a specific communication request subject to certain QoS requirements. If enough resources can be reserved and steadily deployed according to the signaled requirements of a request, the corresponding traffic flow should experience the expected QoS. Hence, BA is a key issue to achieve QoS. In addition, intelligent BA leads to efficient resource utilization which is a general objective of optimal network design [173]. The designing of networks covers many issues like traffic estimation [174], capacity dimensioning [63, 109], multi-hour network design [175–178], routing [21, 138], traffic grooming [143], and combinations of some of these subproblems [179, 180]. It has been studied in literature from many varying perspectives and in the context of many different underlying network technologies.

In particular, the efficiency of various AC methods combined with alternate BA strategies has been compared in many studies [181–183]. Typically, a network topology with predetermined link capacities and a traffic matrix are given. The resulting flow blocking probabilities are simulated or analyzed based on a specified traffic model and serve as a performance measure to compare the different AC/BA approaches. This conventional evaluation has often been applied in the context of call blocking analysis in multi-service ATM networks [110, 176, 184, 185] and also for other multi-layer architectures [186, 187]. To yield more meaningful results than abstract blocking probabilites, we propose a new method to compare different AC/BA approaches by their respective bandwidth requirements. For the sake of simple comparison, we focus on a single

AC approach – the border-to-border budget based network admission control (cf. Sections 3.1.3 and 4.2.2) – and distinguish between the two different BA principles (cf. Section 4.2.1) static bandwidth allocation (SBA) and adaptive bandwidth allocation (ABA). SBA is performed if resources are reserved only once for the entire duration of a communication relationship. In contrast, ABA is performed if the amount of reserved resources is continously adapted according to the current needs of a communication relationship.

4.2 Concept Description of ABA for Capacity Tunnels

Configurable capacity tunnels are a popular means for traffic engineering (TE) in today's Internet. The ATM technology, for instance, deploys this concept as a dual hierarchy of virtual paths and virtual channels [188]. In MPLS and GMPLS, label switched paths (LSPs) are established through a network and associated with a guaranteed bandwidth [167, 189]. Standard protocols [16, 29, 30] set up the tunnels that can be used for bandwidth management and control [190, 191] or network admission control (NAC) purposes. In [63], so-called border-to-border (b2b) budgets (BBBs) represent virtual capacity tunnels through a network. If the tunneling concept and NAC are combined, those BBBs become load-controlled. Per-flow admission control (AC) is then performed only at the ingress routers based on the capacity of the BBBs. An important question in this tunnel-based AC scenario concerns the tunnel sizes, i.e., how much capacity is required by the b2b tunnels to perform fair AC? For static traffic matrices, the answer to this question is given in [192, 193]. For variable traffic matrices, the answer is more complex. Capacity is assigned to the tunnels by either static bandwidth allocation (SBA) or adaptive bandwidth allocation (ABA). In this section, we specify the concept of ABA for capacity tunnels, describe feasible implementations, and provide a new framework to compare the efficiency of ABA to SBA.

4.2.1 Adaptive vs. Static Bandwidth Allocation (SBA)

We consider a network scenario where admission-controlled TE tunnels are established between each ingress/egress router pair (cf. Figure 4.2). If the capacity of a tunnel does not suffice to accommodate another flow, further flows are blocked to ensure that the QoS of flows already admitted to that tunnel is maintained. With SBA, the tunnels have fixed sizes, i.e., they do not adapt to traffic fluctuations. Therefore, they must be dimensioned to cope with the busy-hour traffic which can lead to inefficient use of tunnel-bound network capacity at secondary times. This potential inefficiency can be avoided if ABA is applied to the tunnels, i.e., if the tunnel sizes are dynamically adapted to current traffic conditions. The rearrangement of tunnels is a well known strategy often found in literature [177, 194–196].

In our new performance evaluation framework, the gain of ABA compared to SBA is quantified by bandwidth savings that are achievable with ABA. Given a traffic model, a network topology, and a targeted b2b blocking probability, we calculate the required capacitities for the TE tunnels, compute the corresponding link capacities, and, finally, determine the resulting capacity of the entire network. From our point of view this evaluation method yields more meaningful results with regard to monetary savings than the comparison of abstract blocking probabilities.

4.2.2 Network Requirements

The application of adaptive bandwidth allocation to admission-controlled capacity tunnels imposes certain demands on architecture and functionality of the underlying network as pointed out in the following.

Requirements on Network Architecture

Admission control (AC) is a means to guarantee QoS in terms of limited packet loss and delay for traffic flows. It admits flow requests only if sufficient network resources, e.g. link capacities, are available to carry a new flow in addition to the already admitted flows without QoS violations. Otherwise, the flow is blocked to maintain QoS. When the scope of AC is extended from a single link to an entire network, several fundamental NAC approaches can be categorized (cf. Section 3.1.3). Among them is the BBB NAC which is very resource-efficient, especially if network resilience is taken into account. Due to its technical simplicity and economical superiority, the BBB NAC is integrated in the testbed of the KING (Key components for the Internet of the Next Generation) project [125, 126]. The BBB NAC can be implemented in various technologies using, e.g., MPLS LSPs as single-path capacity tunnels associated with guaranteed bandwidths. To make this MPLS-based system conform with the BBB NAC concept, the LERs at the tunnel ingress must perform AC for their LSPs. In the KING project, the network architecture is purely IP-based and, in contrast to LSPs, the traffic may be carried on multi-paths in this architecture. The BBB NAC is perfectly suitable for that purpose.

For the BBB NAC architecture shown in Figure 4.2, a network $\mathcal{N} = (\mathcal{V}, \mathcal{E})$ is specified by a set of routers $\mathcal{V}$ and a set of links $\mathcal{E}$. BBBs $b_{v,w}$ are defined as capacity tunnels between each two border routers $v, w \in \mathcal{V}$. BBB NAC entities are located at the network egde. They admit new traffic flows $f_{v,w}^{new}$ from v to w recording their requested rates $r_{f_{v,w}^{new}}$ and reject flows if their requested rates exceed the remaining free capacity of $b_{v,w}$. For admission, the following inequality must hold

$$r_{f_{v,w}^{new}} + \sum_{f \in \mathcal{F}_{v,w}} r_f \leq c_{v,w}, \tag{4.1}$$

where $\mathcal{F}_{v,w}$ denotes the set of admitted flows and $c_{v,w}$ is the capacity of the tunnel between nodes v and w. An advantage of the BBB NAC is that it does not induce states to the core of the network. This feature is certainly desired with

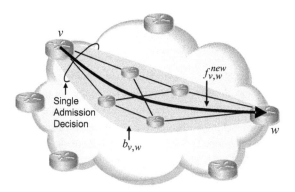

Figure 4.2: *Border-to-border budget based network admission control architecture using multi-path capacity tunnels.*

regard to scalability and resilience. The network capacity assigned to $b_{v,w}$ is exclusively dedicated to the corresponding b2b traffic aggregate $g_{v,w}$ and cannot be used for traffic with different ingress or egress router. Figure 4.2 illustrates that a new flow $f_{v,w}^{new}$ passes only a single AC procedure at the network edge for a specific tunnel $b_{v,w}$. Admitted traffic flows may then be distributed among the partial paths of the illustrated multi-path capacity tunnel from v to w.

Requirements on Network Functionality

Adaptive bandwidth allocation (ABA) adapts the tunnel sizes to the current traffic demands. To trigger the ABA mechanism for the reassignment of tunnel capacities, a qualified feedback from the network about the current traffic load and the corresponding flow blocking probabilities is needed. Basically, both can be acquired through measurements. However, there are two reasons why we do not measure the flow blocking probabilities directly. Firstly, blocking probabilities are usually in the order of 10^{-3} or below and a relatively long time is required to get a good estimate. Secondly, situations with high flow blocking probabilities should be detected before they actually occur in order to avoid them. Instead of observing the flow blocking probabilities directly, we rather observe the time-variant traffic matrix. Traffic matrix estimation is known as a difficult problem [174] but, e.g., label distribution protocol (LDP) [28] statistics provide sufficient means to derive an appropriate estimate of the current traffic matrix [127]. In our case, the BBB NAC entities are supposed to provide the necessary packet counters. The flow blocking probabilities can then be calculated by means of the Kaufman-Roberts algorithm (cf. Section 4.3.1). This method requires instances of the time-variant traffic matrix and a reasonable estimate of the request rate distribution that are obtained from the BBB NAC entities, as well.

An intelligent monitoring entity is required to gather the relevant network information based on which the necessary tunnel capacities are calculated. This entity may also be used to remotely (re-)configure the tunnels in the network. In contrast to, e.g. a bandwidth broker, the entity may be implemented such that it is not vital to normal network operation. If so, the tunnel capacity (re-)assignment can be performed offline and prior to the tunnel (re-)configuration.

4.2.3 Implementation Alternatives

For a static traffic matrix, the virtual capacity tunnels need to be dimensioned only once using SBA. The blocking probabilities for all b2b traffic aggregates are taken for the dimensioning algorithm as target values. If the traffic matrix changes, the current b2b-specific flow blocking probabilities may deviate from these target values, i.e., the flow blocking can increase for some aggregates and decrease for others. The corresponding tunnel capacities may thus become over- or underutilized. ABA solves this problem by continuously adapting the tunnel capacities to changing traffic conditions. In the following, we propose two concepts for the implementation of ABA: (1) complete capacity reassignment (CCR) which reoptimizes all capacity tunnels in the network and (2) selective capacity reassignment (SCR) which adapts only those tunnels that deviate significantly from their planned flow blocking probabilities.

Complete Capacity Reassignment (CCR)

If triggered by some event, the CCR method recalculates and reconfigures all tunnels in the network. There are two options to define such a trigger. The most intuitive is to iterate the CCR in regular time intervals and thus independent of the current network state. An iteration interval that is too small requires much computation power and causes high signaling and configuration costs. An interval that is too long leads to large response times and unnecessary flow blocking. Both extremes must be avoided. An alternative method is to explicitly trigger the CCR whenever the flow blocking probability of one or more tunnels leaves a predefined tolerance interval (TI). Each tunnel has a TI that provides upper and lower bounds for its corresponding flow blocking probability. CCR is triggered only if the current flow blocking probability changes significantly, i.e., if it leaves its TI. The TIs may be defined as, e.g., $TI = [p \cdot exp(-c), p \cdot exp(c)]$, where p is the planned flow blocking probability from the last CCR and c is a deviation parameter which controls the mean time between consecutive CCRs. CCR is thus triggered by a capacity under- or overprovisioning in the tunnels.

Selective Capacity Reassignment (SCR)

The SCR based on the following idea also uses TIs. When the capacity assignment is performed for the first time to initialize the tunnels, a fraction of all link capacities remains unassigned and is retained in a free resource pool (FRP). The flow blocking probabilities resulting from this initial process are considered as target values. If some flow blocking probabilities leave their TIs, only the capacity of affected tunnels is adapted by acquiring more capacity from the FRP or by returning excessive capacity to the FRP. This reduces the overall computation and configuration effort. If the capacity in the FRP is depleted, all budgets are reinitialized. This leads to new target values for the flow blocking probabilities and a fraction of all link capacities is again retained in the FRP.

Comparison of CCR and SCR

Both, complete and selective capacity reassignment adapt the tunnel capacities to the current traffic demands but differ in their implementation, signaling/configuration overhead, and processing complexity. The advantage of SCR over CCR is its fast reaction to a local capacity shortage. However, SCR does not provide the lowest possible blocking probabilities as some available link capacities are not assigned to the tunnels but retained in the FRP. Another disadvantage of SCR is its bad performance in network overload situations when the resources in the FRP are depleted. In this case, it is impossible to shift bandwidth between the tunnels and the blocking probabilities may thus deviate strongly from their target values with large deviations between individual aggregates. A global reinitialization of the tunnels and the FRP can solve this problem.

4.3 Performance Evaluation of ABA for Capacity Tunnels

Conventional performance evaluation of BA/AC methods compares blocking probabilities between alternative implementations. In contrast, our performance analysis rather quantifies bandwidth savings, i.e., network topology, traffic matrix, and target flow blocking probability are given and the required network capacity is calculated. To the best of our knowledge this is the first time in literature that BA/AC methods are compared that way. From our perspective, this kind of comparison leads to more meaningful results for application in practice than the comparison of abstract blocking probabilities. In this section, we illustrate the performance evaluation framework used to compare SBA and ABA for capacity tunnels. An inversion of the Kaufmann & Roberts formula for the computation of blocking probabilities is used to dimension the tunnels. The BA-specific resulting tunnel capacities are subject to economy of scale and determine the overall required network capacity.

4.3.1 Capacity Dimensioning for Virtual Tunnels

When AC is applied, flow requests can be blocked to prevent overload situations. Our goal is to assess the efficiency of ABA vs. SBA for the BBB NAC architecture. Therefore, we compare their respective resource requirements that must be fulfilled to achieve the same blocking probability. The blocking probability is determined by the provisioned capacity and the traffic model. We review our multi-rate Poisson model for real-time traffic and the Kaufman & Roberts formula [82] for the calculation of blocking probabilities. Efficient implementations of this formula and also of its inversion are given in [63]. The inversion yields the capacity dimensioning algorithm for the capacity tunnels and, due to its central meaning, we review it here. Finally, we show that the tunnel capacity requirements are subject to economy of scale and sensitive to various parameters like, e.g. the request size distribution.

A Simple Model for Real-Time Traffic

The underlying traffic model has an essential impact on flow blocking probabilities and on capacity dimensioning. We intend to investigate the BBB NAC with ABA for IP networks which operate on the session level. The inter-arrival time of sessions is exponentially distributed [119]. Therefore, the Poisson model is appropriate for the description of session arrivals which cause reservation requests. It is characterized by an exponentially distributed flow inter-arrival time with rate $\frac{1}{E[A]}$ and an independently and identically distributed flow holding time with mean $E[B]$. The ratio $a = \frac{E[B]}{E[A]}$ is the offered load which equals the mean number of active flows in a system without flow blocking. The offered load is expressed in the pseudo unit Erlang [Erl].

According to the multi-service world of the Internet, a simplified multi-rate model is used to implement the flow request profile for our performance evaluation. The model consists of $n = 3$ different flow request types i, $1 \le i \le n$ with request sizes r_i. The rate of the request-type-specific inter-arrival time distribution and the mean of the flow holding time determine the request-type-specific

request type i	1	2	3
r_i	64 Kbit/s	256 Kbit/s	2048 Kbit/s
$P(\mathcal{R}_\theta = r_i)$	$\frac{28}{31} \cdot \theta^2$	$(1 - \theta^2)$	$\frac{3}{31} \cdot \theta^2$

Table 4.1: *Request type statistics.*

offered load $a_i = \frac{E[B_i]}{E[A_i]}$. The overall load is $a = \sum_{1 \leq i \leq n} a_i$. The random variable $\mathcal{R}_\theta$ indicates the request size in case of a flow arrival and the request size probability is calculated by $P(\mathcal{R}_\theta = r_i) = \frac{E[A]}{E[A_i]}$. The statistical properties of the request types are compiled in Table 4.1. They are chosen such that they yield a constant mean flow request rate of $E[\mathcal{R}_\theta] = 256$ Kbit/s and a coefficient of variation of $c_{var}[\mathcal{R}_\theta] = 2.291 \cdot \theta$ that depends linearly on θ.

The Kaufman & Roberts Formula for the Computation of Blocking Probabilities

An algorithm for the computation of the blocking probabilities for a multi-rate Poisson traffic model has been presented in [82] (18.1.1, p. 516). It is based on discrete capacity units, so we discretize the tunnel bandwidth $c_{v,w}$ into $c_{v,w}^u$ capacity units of size $u_c = 64$ Kbit/s. Analogously, r_i^u is the request rate in capacity units u_c.

Request-Type-Specific Blocking Probabilities   At first, we calculate request-type-specific blocking probabilities $p_b(r_i)$. For that purpose, auxiliary variables $\tilde{w}(j)$ representing state weights for j used capacity units in the tunnel are calculated by

$$
\tilde{w}(j) = \begin{cases} 0 & : j < 0, \\ 1 & : j = 0, \\ \frac{1}{j} \cdot \sum_{1 \leq i \leq n} \tilde{w}(j - r_i^u) \cdot r_i^u \cdot a_i & : 0 < j \leq c_{v,w}^u. \end{cases} \tag{4.2}
$$

A normalization derives the state probabilities $w(j)$ for j used capacity units as

$$w(j) = \tilde{w}(j) \cdot \left(\sum_{k=0}^{c_{v,w}^u} \tilde{w}(k) \right)^{-1}. \qquad (4.3)$$

The request-type-specific blocking probabilities $p_b(r_i)$ depend on the tunnel capacity $c_{v,w}^u$ and are calculated as

$$p_b(r_i) = \sum_{j=c_{v,w}^u - r_i^u + 1}^{c_{v,w}^u} w(j). \qquad (4.4)$$

The above computation model for request-type-specific blocking probabilities takes only the flow level dynamics but not the packet level dynamics into account. If such dynamics are also considered, the request rates can be multiplexed more efficiently in the tunnel. However, packet level dynamics introduce another degree of freedom and complexity. Since we are more interested in NAC than in LAC issues, we use a simple peak rate allocation model.

Aggregate Blocking Probability Flow requests with high rates have a larger blocking probability than those with low rates. For the ease of simple comparison, a single number for the overall aggregate blocking probabilty is required. In [63], AC with trunk reservation (TR) or complete sharing (CS) of resources is considered to obtain aggregate blocking probabilities. Usually, the maximum rate for flow requests is not known in advance and, therefore, TR is not implemented in practice. Hence, CS is used to compute the aggregate blocking probabilties

$$p_b = \sum_{1 \le i \le n} p_b(r_i) \cdot \frac{r_i \cdot P(\mathcal{R}_\theta = r_i)}{E[\mathcal{R}_\theta]}. \qquad (4.5)$$

Equation (4.5) weights the request-type-specific probabilities $P(\mathcal{R}_\theta = r_i)$ with their request sizes r_i. The blocked traffic volume thus corresponds to the aggregate blocking probability p_b.

135

An Efficient Algorithm for Tunnel Capacity Dimensioning

Our performance evaluation framework requires capacity dimensioning which is the inversion of the blocking probability calculation in Equation (4.5). Basically, the tunnel capacity $c_{v,w}^u$ can be increased iteratively until the resulting blocking probability p_{cur} reaches a target blocking probability p_{tar}. This method is computationally expensive. Algorithm 2 calculates the required tunnel capacities much faster by increasing the number j of bandwidth units u_c until the blocking probability p_{cur} is lower than the target blocking probability p_{tar}.

The key idea to accelerate the computation of Algorithm 2 is the introduction of blocking weights $\tilde{p}_b(r_i)$ as auxiliary variables for the request-type-specific blocking probabilities $p(r_i)$. The values $\tilde{p}_b(r_i)$ are incrementally calculated for an increasing tunnel capacity j and serve for the calculation of the probabilities $p(r_i)$. The recursion in Equation (4.2) requires only the storage of c_{max}^u values, where $c_{max}^u = \max_{1 \leq i \leq n} \left(r_i^u \right)$ denotes the maximum request size in capacity units. Therefore, the memory storage for auxiliary variables $\tilde{w}(j)$ can be limited to a cyclic array of size $c_{max}^u + 1$. The utility function STORE($\tilde{w}, j, x$) stores value x associated with index position j in array $\tilde{w}$, GET($\tilde{w}, j$) in Algorithms 3 and 4 recalls the value from index position j of array $\tilde{w}$, and DEVALUATE($\tilde{w}, d$) divides all values in array $\tilde{w}$ by d. To avoid number overflow, downscaling is performed when the control variable T_{ctrl} exceeds a threshold T_{max}.

The function STATEWEIGHTSCS() shown in Algorithm 3 computes the state weights $\tilde{w}$ as defined in Equation (4.2) and also the incremental weight T_{add}. The latter variable is used in the function BLOCKINGWEIGHTSCS() which calculates the request-type-specific blocking weights $\tilde{p}_b(r_i)$ as shown in Algorithm 4. Finally, the function BLOCKINGPROBABILITY() calculates the aggregate blocking probability p_{cur}, which is used as stop criterion for the iterative tunnel capacity increase. The details of this function are omitted but can be found in [63].

Input: target blocking probability p_{tar}, request type information

$j := 0$ {initialization}
if $\sum_{1 \leq i \leq n} a_i > 0$ **then**
  STORE$(\tilde{w}, 0, 1)$ {$\tilde{w}(0) := 1$}
  for $0 < k \leq c_{max}^u$ **do**   {initialization}
    STORE$(\tilde{w}, k, 0)$ {$\tilde{w}(k) := 0$}
  end for
  for $1 \leq i \leq n$ **do**   {initialization}
    $\tilde{p}_b(r_i) := 1$
  end for
  $p_{cur} := 1; T_{ctrl} := 1$ {$T_{ctrl} := \sum_{k=0}^{j} \tilde{w}(k)$}
  while $p_{cur} > p_{tar}$ **do**   {until blocking probability is small enough}
    if $T_{ctrl} > T_{max}$ **then**   {scale down if numbers become too large}
      for $1 \leq i \leq n$ **do**
        $\tilde{p}_b(r_i) := \frac{\tilde{p}_b(r_i)}{T_{ctrl}}$
      end for
      DEVALUATE$(\tilde{w}, T_{ctrl}); T_{ctrl} := 1$
    end if
    $j := j + 1$
    $(\tilde{w}, T_{add}) :=$ STATEWEIGHTSCS$(j, \tilde{w})$
    $T_{ctrl} := T_{ctrl} + T_{add}$
    $p_{cur} := 0$ {p_{cur} is updated}
    for $1 \leq i \leq n$ **do**
      $\tilde{p}_b(r_i) :=$ BLOCKINGWEIGHTSCS$(\tilde{p}_b(r_i), i, \tilde{w}, j, T_{add})$
    end for
    $p_b(r_i) := \frac{\tilde{p}_b(r_i)}{T_{ctrl}}$
    $p_{cur} :=$ BLOCKINGPROBABILITIY$(j,$ request type information$)$
  end while
end if

Output: required capacity units j

Algorithm 2: CAPACITYDIMENSIONING: computation of required bandwidth for border-to-border capacity tunnels.

Input: $j, \tilde{w}, T_{ctrl}$, request type information

$x := 0$ {computes $\tilde{w}(j)$ according to Equation (4.2)}
for $1 \leq i \leq n$ **do**
$\quad x := x + \text{GET}(\tilde{w}, j - r_i^u) \cdot r_i^u \cdot a_i$
end for
$x := \frac{x}{j}$; store$(\tilde{w}, j, x)$ {$\tilde{w}(j) := x$}

Output: state weights $\tilde{w}$, weight increment x

Algorithm 3: STATEWEIGHTSCS: computation of state weights for CS.

Input: $\tilde{p}_b(r_i), i, \tilde{w}, j, T_{add}$, request type information

$\tilde{p}_b(r_i) := \tilde{p}_b(r_i) - \text{GET}(\tilde{w}, j - r_i^u) + T_{add}$

Output: request-type-specific blocking weights $\tilde{p}_b(r_i)$

Algorithm 4: BLOCKINGWEIGHTSCS: computation of request-type-specific blocking weights for CS.

Economy of Scale of Tunnel Sizes

The tunnel capacity dimensioning performed in Algorithm 2 is sensitive to different network parameters and traffic characteristics such as offered load, request rate variability, and targeted aggregate blocking probability. Variations of these parameters influence the required tunnel capacity and the corresponding resource utilization and lead to the phenomenon of economy of scale.

Impact of Offered Load and Request Rate Variability

We dimension the required tunnel capacity $c_{v,w}$ for a targeted aggregate blocking probability of $p_b = 10^{-3}$ and vary the load $a_{v,w}$ that is offered to the tunnel. In addition, the impact of the request rate variability $\mathcal{R}_\theta$ (cf. Table 4.1) is investigated by setting its interpolation parameter to values of $\theta \in \{0, 1\}$, respectively.

Figures 4.3(a) and 4.3(b) show the required tunnel capacity $c_{v,w}$ and the corresponding resource utilization $\rho = \frac{c_{v,w}}{a_{v,w} \cdot E[\mathcal{R}_\theta]}$ for different offered loads $a_{v,w}$ and request size distributions $\mathcal{R}_0$ and $\mathcal{R}_1$. The required capacity is almost proportional to the offered load, at least for a value of $a_{v,w} = 10^3$ Erl or larger. The resource utilization is a measure for the efficiency of the capacity tunnel. The fact that little offered load leads to low utilization and that large offered load leads to high utilization is a non-linear functional dependency which is called economy of scale or multiplexing gain.

Regarding the request size variability $\mathcal{R}_\theta$, the resource utilization emphasizes the difference between the distributions with parameters $\theta \in \{0, 1\}$ more visibly than the required capacity. Increasing the request rate variability increases the required capacity and decreases the resource efficiency but only to a limited extent that vanishes for high offered load. In the following investigations, we use the request size distribution $\mathcal{R}_1$ as default since traffic in the future Internet is expected to be more variable than in the ISDN telephone network whose 64 Kbit/s connections correspond to $\mathcal{R}_0$.

Impact of Blocking Probability Figures 4.4(a) and 4.4(b) illustrate the influence of different aggregate blocking probabilities $p_b \in \{10^{-1}, 10^{-3}, 10^{-5}\}$ and the offered load $a_{v,w}$ on the required tunnel capacity $c_{v,w}$ and the resource utilization ρ for request rate distribution $\mathcal{R}_1$. Economy of scale is observed for all curves but larger blocking probabilities allow for a visibly better resource utilization. However, this influence decreases for high offered load and the resource utilization eventually converges for all blocking probabilities to 100%. Regarding the capacity curves in Figure 4.4(a), the difference among the alternative blocking probabilities is hardly visible for values of $a_{v,w} = 10^4$ Erl or larger. If not mentioned differently, a target aggregate blocking probability of $p_b = 10^{-3}$ is used in the following.

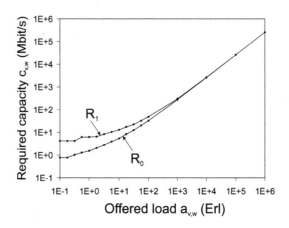

(a) Impact on required tunnel capacity.

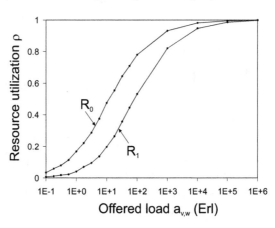

(b) Impact on tunnel resource utilization.

Figure 4.3: *Impact of offered load and rate variability on required tunnel capacity and resource utilization.*

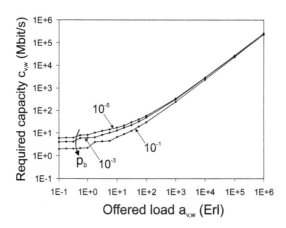

(a) Impact on required tunnel capacity.

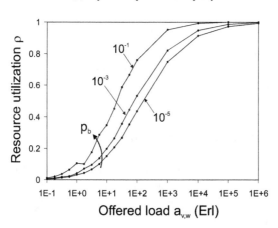

(b) Impact on tunnel resource utilization.

Figure 4.4: *Impact of offered load and target aggregate blocking probability on required tunnel capacity and resource utilization.*

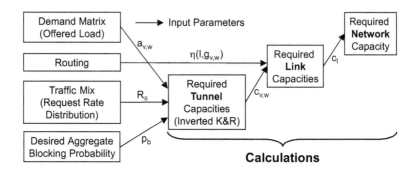

Figure 4.5: *Calculation steps for determining the required network capacity.*

4.3.2 Network Dimensioning with SBA and ABA

We derive general formulae for the calculation of the required network capacity which serves as performance measure for the comparison of SBA and ABA. For each BA method, the specific procedure for determining the network capacity requirements is considered.

General Dimensioning Approach

To determine the required network capacity, we assume a common targeted aggregate blocking probability p_b. Firstly, the required tunnel capacities are calculated based on the probability p_b, the request rate distribution $\mathcal{R}_\theta$, and the offered loads $a_{v,w}$ of the b2b traffic aggregates. The resulting tunnel capacities $c_{v,w}$ and the pre-determined routing information $\eta(l, g_{v,w})$ are then used to compute the minimum required link capacities c_l. Summing up these link capacities finally yields the overall required network capacity. An overview of the calculation steps is given in Figure 4.5.

Calculation of the Required Tunnel Capacities The offered load for a b2b traffic aggregate $g_{v,w} \in \mathcal{G}$ is denoted by $a_{v,w}$. The resulting matrix $A_{\mathcal{G}} = [a_{v,w}]_{v,w \in \mathcal{V}}$ is the traffic demand matrix. Algorithm 2 calculates the required tunnel capacities $c_{v,w}$ based on the b2b offered loads $a_{v,w}$, the request rate distribution $\mathcal{R}_\theta$, and the targeted aggregate blocking probability p_b.

Calculation of the Required Link Capacities The admitted rate of a b2b aggregate $g_{v,w}$ is given by $r_{v,w}$ and the matrix $C_{\mathcal{G}} = [r_{v,w}]_{v,w \in \mathcal{V}}$ describes a network-wide admitted traffic pattern. Each possible traffic pattern $C_{\mathcal{G}} \in \mathbb{R}_0^{+|\mathcal{V}|^2}$ obeys to the following formulae

$$\forall v, w \in \mathcal{V}: \quad r_{v,w} \geq 0 \tag{4.6}$$

$$\forall v \in \mathcal{V}: \quad r_{v,v} = 0. \tag{4.7}$$

If BBB NAC is applied to the network, the traffic patterns must additionally satisfy the constraints imposed by the tunnel capacities $c_{v,w}$ (cf. Equation (4.1)), i.e. the inequation

$$\forall v, w \in \mathcal{V}: \quad r_{v,w} \leq c_{v,w} \tag{4.8}$$

must hold. To determine the minimum required link capacity c_l for each link $l \in \mathcal{E}$, a worst case analysis is performed that uses Equations (4.6) – (4.8) as side conditions in the capacity minimization

$$c_l \geq \sum_{v,w \in \mathcal{V}} c_{v,w} \cdot \eta(l, g_{v,w}), \tag{4.9}$$

where function $\eta(l, g_{v,w})$ represents the routing information and denotes the portion of aggregate $g_{v,w}$ that is transported on link l. In case of single path routing, we have $\eta(l, g_{v,w}) \in \{0, 1\}$ whereas, for multi-path routing, $\eta(l, g_{v,w}) \in \mathbb{R}_0^+$ is possible.

Calculation of the Required Network Capacity The overall required network capacity is our primary performance measure and simply defined as the sum

$$C_{tot} = \sum_{l \in \mathcal{E}} c_l \qquad (4.10)$$

over all required link capacities c_l. Now that we have described the general approch to network dimensioning, we adopt this procedure to derive dimensioning methods that are specific to SBA and ABA, respectively.

Network Dimensioning with SBA

The general network dimensioning approach assumes a static demand matrix. For the performance comparison of SBA and ABA, however, the b2b traffic aggregates are supposed to be variable over time which yields time-variant demand matrices. If the b2b tunnels are dimensioned with SBA, the demand matrix $\mathcal{A}_{max} = [max_t(a_{v,w}(t))]_{v,w \in \mathcal{V}}$ contains for each aggregate $g_{v,w}$ its maximum offered load over all time instances t. Hence, the busy hour traffic aggregates must be supported by the tunnels with statically assigned capacity. For SBA, the capacity c_l^{SBA} of link l is then calculated as the sum of capacities of those tunnels whose aggregates are carried on l. Finally, we calculate the overall required network capacity C_{tot}^{SBA} for SBA based on the demand matrix $\mathcal{A}_{max}$ as

$$C_{tot}^{SBA} = \sum_{l \in \mathcal{E}} c_l^{SBA}. \qquad (4.11)$$

Network Dimensioning with ABA

In contrast to SBA, ABA continuously adapts the capacity tunnel sizes to the demand variations of the corresponding traffic aggregates. To reach that goal, the network is reoptimized in certain time intervals (cf. Section 4.2.3). More precisely, the tunnels are redimensioned based on the time-dependent demand matrices $\mathcal{A}(t)$ which yields time-dependent link capacities $c_l(t)$. For ABA, the actually required link capacity c_l^{ABA} of link l is then defined as the maximum of all link capacities $c_l(t)$ over all times t, i.e. $c_l^{ABA} = max_t(c_l(t))$. Finally, we calculate the sum C_{tot}^{ABA} of the link capacities c_l^{ABA} as the overall required network capacity for ABA as

$$C_{tot}^{ABA} = \sum_{l \in \mathcal{E}} c_l^{ABA}. \tag{4.12}$$

Summary

We have illustrated the performance evaluation framework used to compare SBA and ABA for capacity tunnels. Assuming a simple multi-rate traffic model and a certain blocking probability for flow requests, the capacity tunnels are dimensioned using an algorithm that inverts the Kaufmann & Roberts formula for the computation of blocking probabilities. The required tunnel capacity and the corresponding resource utilization are sensitive to the request rate variability, the blocking probability, and, in particular, to the traffic load offered to the tunnel. The measure to compare the performance of SBA and ABA is the overall network capacity required by each BA method, respectively. Therefore, a general network dimensioning approach is presented from which the specific dimensioning methods for SBA and ABA are derived.

4.4 Impact of Traffic Demand Models on ABA Bandwidth Savings

The benefits of ABA over SBA are potential bandwidth savings that can be achieved if the traffic demand matrix is variable over time and the tunnel sizes are adapted accordingly. With SBA, the capacity of a tunnel must be dimensioned for its busy hour. At secondary times, this capacity is underutilized if the load offered to the tunnel is significantly lower. If the busy hours of different b2b traffic aggregates occur at different times, some of the bandwidth of underutilized tunnels can be used to support other tunnels in their busy hour. This change in current tunnel capacity requirements leads to bandwidth savings.

In the following, we illustrate the impact of traffic demand models on the bandwidth savings achievable with ABA. At first, static demand matrices proportional to city sizes are constructed. These matrices are then made time-variant such that they yield an opportunistic demand model allowing for maximum bandwidth savings. More realistic demand models for wide area networks (WANs) are constructed proportional to the user activities at the network nodes. For all resulting demand matrices, the overall traffic in the network remains constant. A concluding single link analysis reveals how bandwidth savings become possible. Some of the results are published in [197, 198].

4.4.1 Modelling of Static Demands

For the construction of static traffic demand matrices, we consider a network structure described by a graph notation. A network topology is specified by a tuple $\mathcal{N} = (\mathcal{V}, \mathcal{E})$, where the set of vertices $\mathcal{V}$ contains all routers and the set of edges $\mathcal{E}$ contains all uni-directional links. In our experiments, each node $v \in \mathcal{V}$ is associated with a city. The overall offered network load $a_{tot} = a_{b2b} \cdot |\mathcal{V}| \cdot (|\mathcal{V}| - 1)$ is defined based on the average b2b offered load a_{b2b} and the number of network nodes $|\mathcal{V}|$. For each pair of ingress/egress nodes v and w, we define a static offered load

$$a_{v,w} = \begin{cases} \frac{a_{tot} \cdot \pi(v) \cdot \pi(w)}{\sum_{x,y \in \mathcal{V}, x \neq y} \pi(x) \cdot \pi(y)} & \text{if } v \neq w \\ 0 & \text{if } v = w \end{cases}, \quad (4.13)$$

where $\pi(v)$ is the population of the city associated with node $v \in \mathcal{V}$. The values $a_{v,w}$ and thus the entire static traffic demand matrix can be scaled by the setting of a_{b2b}. Please note that the demand matrix $\mathcal{A} = [a_{v,w}]_{v,w \in \mathcal{V}}$ merely contains the offered loads measured in Erlang between each two tunnel endpoints. To get an instantaneous traffic pattern, the loads $a_{v,w}$ must be multiplied with the mean value of the flow request size distribution which is set to 256 Kbit/s (cf. Table 4.1).

4.4.2 Dynamic Opportunistic Demand Model

Model Description

Time-variant traffic matrices are a prerequisite to effectively apply ABA which is most effective if busy and idle hours of various b2b aggregates complement each other on a single link. Based on the static demands derived in Equation (4.13), we use squared sine and cosine functions with a 24-hour period to model time-variant demand matrices with a maximum potential for bandwidth savings. These matrices are constructed such that the overall offered load in the network remains constant. For an optimal complementation of busy and idle times of the aggregates composed on a single link, we exploit the correlation $\forall t \in \mathbb{R} : \sin^2(t) + \cos^2(t) = 1$ and set the offered loads $a_{v,w}(t)$ according to Equation (4.14). The variables $a'_{v,w}$ and $w_{v,w}$ are calculated by Algorithm 5.

$$a_{v,w}(t) = \begin{cases} 2 \cdot a'_{v,w} \cdot \sin^2(t) & \text{if } v \neq w \wedge w_{v,w} = 0 \\ 2 \cdot a'_{v,w} \cdot \cos^2(t) & \text{if } v \neq w \wedge w_{v,w} = 1 \\ 0 & \text{if } v = w \end{cases} \quad (4.14)$$

147

Input: topology, routing, and static traffic matrix $\mathcal{A}[a_{v,w}]_{v,w \in \mathcal{V}}$

$\mathcal{G}_{hot} := \{g_{v,w} : (v,w) \in \mathcal{V} \times \mathcal{V}\}$
while $\mathcal{G}_{hot} \neq \emptyset$ **do**
   choose aggregate $g_{v,w}^* \in \mathcal{G}_{hot}$ with longest path
   $\delta_{max} := 0$
   for all l used by $g_{v,w}^*$ **do**
      $\delta := |\Sigma_l^{sin} - \Sigma_l^{cos}|$
      if $\delta > \delta_{max}$ **then**
         if $\Sigma_l^{cos} > \Sigma_l^{sin}$ **then**
            $\omega_{tmp} := 0$
         else
            $\omega_{tmp} := 1$
         end if
         $\delta_{max} := \delta$
      end if
   end for
   $\omega_{v,w} := \omega_{tmp}$
   if $g_{v,w}^*$ uses only one link **then**
      $a_{v,w}' := \delta_{max}$
   else
      $a_{v,w}' := a_{v,w}$
   end if
   for all links l used by $g_{v,w}^*$ **do**
      if $\omega_{tmp} = 0$ **then**
         $\Sigma_l^{sin} := \Sigma_l^{sin} + a_{v,w}'$
      else
         $\Sigma_l^{cos} := \Sigma_l^{cos} + a_{v,w}'$
      end if
   end for
end while

Output: $a_{v,w}'$ and $\omega_{v,w}$

Algorithm 5: OPPORTUNISTICDEMANDS: computation of opportunistic demand oscillations for maximum bandwidth savings.

Algorithm 5 assigns to any b2b aggregate $g_{v,w}$ an offered load $a'_{v,w}$ and an oscillation type $\omega_{v,w} \in \{sin, cos\}$. For that purpose, it records for any link $l \in \mathcal{E}$ the sums Σ_l^{sin} and Σ_l^{cos} of the link loads oscillating with either sine or cosine. The value $a'_{v,w}$ is set to the offered load of the aggregate $g^*_{v,w}$ with the longest path in the set of yet undetermined aggregates $\mathcal{G}_{hot}$. Within this path, the link l with the largest difference $\delta = |\Sigma_l^{sin} - \Sigma_l^{cos}|$ is selected. If Σ_l^{cos} is larger than Σ_l^{sin}, the oscillation type of the considered aggregate is set to sin and, otherwise, to cos. This procedure is repeated for all aggregates that are routed over more than one link. In general, the two sums Σ_l^{sin} and Σ_l^{cos} cannot be matched exactly when the oscillation types and traffic loads are set as previously described, i.e., the busy and idle hours of the aggregates on link l are not completely complementary. To achieve absolute balance, the oscillation type and the offered load of the aggregate routed only on l and on no other link is set to the difference $|\Sigma_l^{sin} - \Sigma_l^{cos}|$.

ABA Performance Evaluation

We dimension the test network shown in Figure 4.6 with the city populations given in Table 4.2 for the previously defined opportunistic traffic demand model and for different offered loads a_{b2b}. The rate request distribution is $\mathcal{R}_1$ and the blocking probability is set to $p_b = 10^{-3}$. Using SBA, we dimension the capacity tunnels only once for the peak load demand matrix $\mathcal{A}_{max}$ and sum up the resulting link capacities c_l^{SBA} to the overall required network capacity $\mathcal{C}_{tot}^{SBA}$. For ABA, the tunnel sizes are optimized every 5 minutes during a 24 hours day cycle, i.e., the capacity tunnels are redimensioned based on the dynamic traffic demand matrices $\mathcal{A}(t = i \cdot 5$ min$)$ which yields time-dependent link capacities $c_l(t)$. The actually required link capacity is the maximum of required link capacities over all times t, i.e. $c_l^{ABA} = max_{t \in [0:00, \, 24:00)}(c_l(t))$. Finally, we calculate the sum $\mathcal{C}_{tot}^{ABA}$ of the maximum link capacities c_l^{ABA} as the overall required network capacity for ABA.

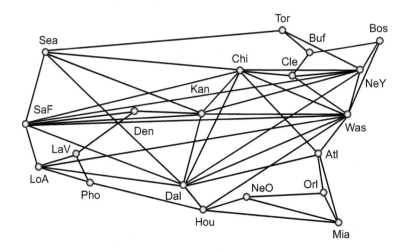

Figure 4.6: *Test network topology for opportunistic demand model evaluation.*

Name(v)	$\pi(v)[10^3]$	Name(v)	$\pi(v)[10^3]$
Atlanta (**Atl**)	4112	Los Angeles (**LoA**)	9519
Boston (**Bos**)	3407	Miami (**Mia**)	2253
Buffalo (**Buf**)	1170	New Orleans (**NeO**)	1338
Chicago (**Chi**)	8273	New York (**NeY**)	9314
Cleveland (**Cle**)	2250	Orlando (**Orl**)	1645
Dallas (**Dal**)	3519	Phoenix (**Pho**)	3252
Denver (**Den**)	2109	San Francisco (**SaF**)	1731
Houston (**Hou**)	4177	Seattle (**Sea**)	2414
Kansas (**Kan**)	1776	Toronto (**Tor**)	4680
Las Vegas (**LaV**)	1536	Washington (**Was**)	4923

Table 4.2: *City populations for opportunistic demand model evaluation.*

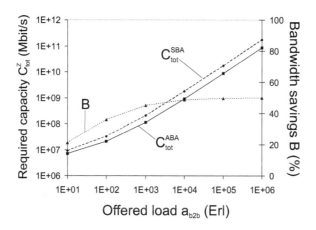

Figure 4.7: *Network capacity requirements and bandwidth savings for opportunistic demand variations.*

Numerical Results   Figure 4.7 shows the numerical results of our experiments for different offered loads a_{b2b} and BA methods $Z \in \{SBA, ABA\}$. The overall required network capacities $\mathcal{C}_{tot}^{SBA}$ and $\mathcal{C}_{tot}^{ABA}$ both increase almost linearly with rising loads a_{b2b}. As expected, more capacity is required for SBA than for ABA which can be clearly observed by the resulting bandwidth savings $\mathcal{B} = 1 - \mathcal{C}_{tot}^{ABA} / \mathcal{C}_{tot}^{SBA}$.

Our experiments were designed such that bandwidth savings of 50% could be expected with ABA compared to SBA. However, the results show that the bandwidth savings strongly depend on the offered load a_{b2b}. The expected savings can be achieved only for sufficiently high values $a_{b2b} \geq 10^4$ Erl while for low offered loads like $a_{b2b} = 10$ Erl, only half of the bandwidth savings potential can be exploited. This behavior is due to the economy of scale that depends on the tunnel sizes, i.e., for a given blocking probability, the required tunnel capacities are on average less utilized for low offered load than for high offered load.

With SBA, the capacity of a tunnel is always dimensioned for the maximum offered load of its b2b aggregate. Hence, this capacity can be utilized to a relatively large degree. With ABA, the load $a_{v,w}(t)$ offered to a tunnel can be very small. The corresponding tunnel capacity is smaller and, hence, it is used on average to a minor degree. However, if the offered load a_{b2b} is sufficiently high, the tunnel capacities for ABA are large enough such that a good resource utilization is achieved. This explains the convergence of the bandwidth savings $\mathcal{B}$ to 50% for larger values a_{b2b}.

Of course, the amount of bandwidth saved with ABA (up to 50% of SBA) is due to the specific construction of the time-variant demand matrices. In general, the bandwidth savings potential depends on the request rate distribution and the variability of the network traffic over the time of the day. It can be exploited best if the offered load in the network is high like, e.g., in wide area networks.

4.4.3 Dynamic Demand Models for Wide Area Networks

In local area networks (LANs), the busy hours of all traffic aggregates are supposed to coincide. It is thus unlikely that one capacity tunnel is overloaded while another one is underutilized. This is different in wide area networks (WANs) because the busy hours of individual traffic aggregates depend on the time zones in which the corresponding endpoint routers are located. Therefore, ABA should be applied to the capacity tunnels to achieve bandwidth savings in WANs.

Model Description

For the construction of dynamic demand matrices for WANs, we define a function that calculates the online activity of a city population. This function assigns to each node $v \in \mathcal{V}$ an activity factor $\gamma_v(t)$ which depends on the coordinated

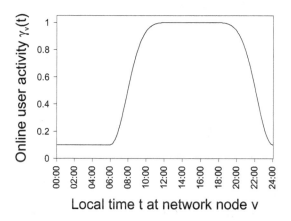

Figure 4.8: *Online user activity at a network node over 24h.*

universal time (UTC) t and the time zone of node v and which is calculated as

$$\gamma_v(t) = \begin{cases} 0.1 & \text{if } \mathcal{L}(v,t) \in [0{:}00, 6{:}00) \\ 1 - 0.9 \cdot \left(\cos \left(\frac{(\mathcal{L}(v,t)-6h)\pi}{18h} \right) \right)^{10} & \text{else.} \end{cases}$$

(4.15)

The function $\mathcal{L}(v,t) = (t + \tau(v) + 24) \bmod 24 \; \forall t \in [0{:}00, 24{:}00)$ calculates the local time at node $v \in \mathcal{V}$ at UTC t with $\tau(v)$ being the time zone offset of node v. The activity function $\gamma_v(t)$ is illustrated in Figure 4.8. The curve shows the percentage of active users among the population of node v depending on the local time t.

Based on the online user activities at network nodes v and w, three simple options for the fluctuation of aggregate loads $a_{v,w}(t)$ over time t can be identified. The traffic demand matrices derived from these options are made time-variant such that the overall offered load in the network remains constant.

Linearity to Provider Activity (LPA)   With the LPA demand model, the offered load $a_{v,w}(t)$ of aggregate $g_{v,w}$ is proportional to the online user activity at the traffic-providing node v :

$$a_{v,w}(t) = \begin{cases} \frac{a_{tot} \cdot \pi(v) \cdot \gamma_v(t) \cdot \pi(w)}{\sum_{x,y \in \mathcal{V}, x \neq y} \pi(x) \cdot \gamma_x(t) \cdot \pi(y)} & \text{if } v \neq w \\ 0 & \text{if } v = w \end{cases} \quad \forall t \in [0{:}00, 24{:}00)$$

(4.16)

Demand fluctuations following the LPA model may be caused by client-server applications, where the clients are triggered by human beings and push content to a server, e.g. for data backup purposes.

Linearity to Consumer Activity (LCA)   With the LCA demand model, the offered load $a_{v,w}(t)$ of aggregate $g_{v,w}$ is proportional to the online user activity at the traffic-consuming node w:

$$a_{v,w}(t) = \begin{cases} \frac{a_{tot} \cdot \pi(v) \cdot \pi(w) \cdot \gamma_w(t)}{\sum_{x,y \in \mathcal{V}, x \neq y} \pi(x) \cdot \pi(y) \cdot \gamma_y(t)} & \text{if } v \neq w \\ 0 & \text{if } v = w \end{cases} \quad \forall t \in [0{:}00, 24{:}00)$$

(4.17)

Demand fluctuations following the LCA model may be caused by client-server applications, where the clients pull content from a server, e.g. for web downloads. The LCA and LPA model provide similar demand matrices and, therefore, we consider only LCA in the following.

Linearity to Provider and Consumer Activity (LPCA)   With the LPCA demand model, the offered load $a_{v,w}(t)$ of aggregate $g_{v,w}$ is proportional to the online user activities at both endpoints v and w of the aggregate:

$$a_{v,w}(t) = \begin{cases} \frac{a_{tot} \cdot \pi(v) \cdot \gamma_v(t) \cdot \pi(w) \cdot \gamma_w(t)}{\sum_{x,y \in \mathcal{V}, x \neq y} \pi(x) \cdot \gamma_x(t) \cdot \pi(y) \cdot \gamma_y(t)} & \text{if } v \neq w \\ 0 & \text{if } v = w \end{cases} \quad \forall t \in [0{:}00, 24{:}00)$$

(4.18)

Name(v)	$\pi(v)$	$\tau(v)$	Name(v)	$\pi(v)$	$\tau(v)$
Honolulu	378.155	-11	Athens *	745.514	+2
Los Angeles *	3.798.981	-8	Helsinki *	1.027.305	+2
Vancouver *	545.671	-8	Moscow *	10.101.500	+3
Denver *	560.415	-7	New Delhi	12.791.458	+4
Chicago *	2.886.251	-6	Bangkok	6.320.174	+6
Houston *	2.009.834	-6	Beijing	13.820.000	+7
New York *	8.084.316	-5	Hong Kong	6.708.389	+7
Toronto *	2.481.494	-5	Singapore	4.017.733	+7
London *	6.638.109	0	Seoul	9.895.972	+8
Berlin *	3.388.434	+1	Tokyo	8.134.688	+8
Cape Town	2.415.408	+1	Melbourne	3.366.542	+9
München *	1.227.958	+1	Sydney	3.997.321	+9
Paris *	2.125.246	+1	Auckland	406.000	+11

Table 4.3: *City populations and time zones for WAN demand model evaluation (* summertime).*

Demand fluctuations following the LPCA model may be caused by peer-to-peer applications, where content is exchanged among peers that are controlled by human beings. The peers may request and offer contents at the same time. Another application is IP telephony with and without video support based on, e.g. the session initiation protocol (SIP).

ABA Performance Evaluation

We dimension the test network shown in Figure 4.9. The nodes are located in different time zones which, together with the population of the associated cities and their surroundings, are compiled in Table 4.3. The bandwidth savings achievable with ABA are evaluated for the previously defined LCA and LPCA traffic demand models for different offered loads a_{b2b}. The rate request distribution is $\mathcal{R}_1$ and the blocking probability is set to $p_b = 10^{-3}$. The overall required network capacities for SBA and ABA are calculated according to Equations (4.11) and (4.12), respectively.

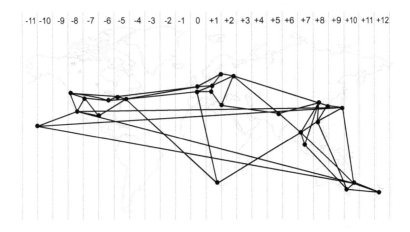

| -11 | -10 | -9 | -8 | -7 | -6 | -5 | -4 | -3 | -2 | -1 | 0 | +1 | +2 | +3 | +4 | +5 | +6 | +7 | +8 | +9 | +10 | +11 | +12 |

Figure 4.9: *Test network topology for WAN demand model evaluation.*

Numerical Results   Our performance measures are the overall required network capacity C_Y^Z and the resulting bandwidth savings $\mathcal{B}_Y$ calculated for all combinations of WAN traffic demand model $Y \in \{LCA, LPCA\}$ and BA method $Z \in \{SBA, ABA\}$. Figure 4.10(a) shows the required capacities C_{LCA}^Z and the bandwidth savings $\mathcal{B}_{LCA}$ as a function of the offered load a_{b2b} for the LCA traffic demand model. Figure 4.10(b) accordingly shows the results C_{LPCA}^Z and $\mathcal{B}_{LPCA}$ for the LPCA model.

Obviously, the required network capacities of both BA methods scale almost linearly with increasing offered load since both axes, i.e. the x-axis and the primary y-axis, use a logarithmic scale. In Figure 4.10(a), the capacity curves C_{LCA}^{SBA} and and C_{LCA}^{ABA} almost coincide. The bandwidth savings $\mathcal{B}_{LCA}$ are shown as a dotted curve on the linearly scaled secondary y-axis. For the LCA traffic demand model, almost no bandwidth savings $\mathcal{B}_{LCA} \approx 2\%$ are achievable with ABA.

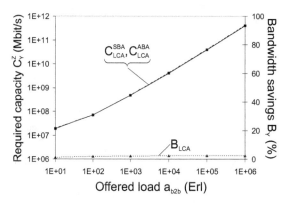

(a) LCA traffic demand model.

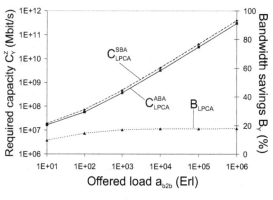

(b) LPCA traffic demand model.

Figure 4.10: *Network capacity requirements and bandwidth savings for demand variations in WANs.*

In Figure 4.10(b), the capacity curves $\mathcal{C}_{LPCA}^{SBA}$ and $\mathcal{C}_{LPCA}^{ABA}$ are clearly visible as separate lines. Hence, more bandwidth $\mathcal{B}_{LPCA} \approx 18\%$ can be saved if the LPCA model is assumed. For this traffic demand model, the achievable bandwidth savings depend on the offered load a_{b2b} and siginificant savings are realized only for sufficiently high offered loads $a_{b2b} \geq 10^4$ Erl. Figure 4.10(b) also shows that the bandwidth savings $\mathcal{B}_{LPCA}$ stabilize with increasing offered load.

To understand this behavior, we study the capacity requirements of individual links for both WAN demand models over 24 hours. Figures 4.11(a) and 4.11(b) show them for links Seoul $\rightarrow$ Tokyo and Bangkok $\rightarrow$ Beijing for the LCA model and Figures 4.12(a) and 4.12(b) show them for LPCA. The depicted curves result for an offered load $a_{b2b} = 10^4$ Erl. For both links, the maximum required link capacities $\mathcal{C}_{LCA}^Z$ shown in Figures 4.11(a) and 4.11(b) are about the same for SBA and ABA. The LPCA model allows for bandwidth savings $\mathcal{B}_{LPCA} \approx 46\%$ on the link Seoul $\rightarrow$ Tokyo (cf. Figure 4.12(a)) if ABA is used instead of SBA. In contrast, much less bandwidth can be saved for this demand model on the link Bangkok $\rightarrow$ Beijing (cf. Figure 4.12(b)). A comparison between LCA and LPCA with regard to their busy hour period lengths shows that the maximum link capacity for LCA is required on average over a longer time than for LPCA.

The effects on the amount of bandwidth savings can be explained by further analyzing the traffic composed of different b2b aggregates on a single link l. Each aggregate has its own time-dependent capacity requirements that are superposed for all aggregates transported on l. The LCA model leads to longer busy hour periods than the LPCA model and this propagates to the time-dependent capacity requirements of link l. The shorter busy hour periods of LPCA are more likely to occur temporally displaced and the reduced overlapping of busy hours decreases the maximum required link capacity for ABA. This is well observable on the link Seoul $\rightarrow$ Tokyo that carries 30 different traffic aggregates with busy hours at different times. In contrast, the link Bangkok $\rightarrow$ Beijing supports only 22 different aggregates whose busy hours coincide for both WAN demand models. Hence, ABA achieves significant capacity savings only if the busy hour periods of the traffic aggregates on a link do not overlap.

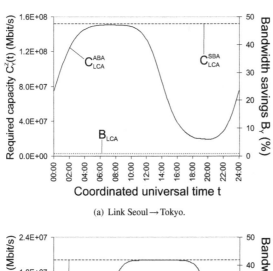

(a) Link Seoul → Tokyo.

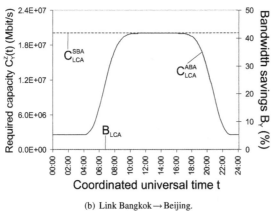

(b) Link Bangkok → Beijing.

Figure 4.11: *Link capacity requirements and bandwidth savings for the LCA traffic demand model.*

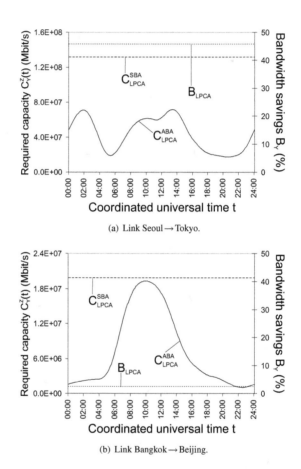

(a) Link Seoul → Tokyo.

(b) Link Bangkok → Beijing.

Figure 4.12: *Link capacity requirements and bandwidth savings for the LPCA traffic demand model.*

Summary

We have illustrated the impact of different traffic demand models on the bandwidth savings achievable with ABA. Our analytical results show that the demand model assumed for network dimensioning has a major impact on the bandwidth savings potential of ABA. To generate traffic demands, static traffic demand matrices are constructed proportionally to city sizes. These matrices are made time-variant such that the overall offered load in the network remains constant. For variable b2b traffic aggregates oscillating opportunistically on all network links, the maximum bandwidth savings of 50% are only achieved if the offered load in the network is high enough. More realistic traffic demand models for wide area networks (WANs) are constructed proportionally to the user activities at the network nodes which yields three different models: linearity to provider activity (LPA), linearity to consumer activity (LCA), and linearity to provider and consumer activity (LPCA). For a target aggregate blocking probability $p_b = 10^{-3}$ and the flow request size distribution $\mathcal{R}_1$, bandwidth savings are hardly achievable with LPA/LCA ($\approx$ 2%), whereas more significant savings ($\approx$ 18%) are obtained with the LPCA model. A single link analysis reveals that bandwidth savings with ABA depend on the overlapping of busy hours of aggregates compiled on a link. Bandwidth savings are increased if these busy periods occur at different times. Routing and load balancing have a significant impact on the compilation of traffic transported on a single link. This gives room to further investigations as illustrated in the next section.

4.5 Impact of Tunnel Implementations on ABA Bandwidth Savings

In this section, we consider ABA for different implementations of capacity tunnels. Previously, the impact of traffic demand models on the bandwidth savings achievable with ABA is investigated for single path capacity tunnels only. Now these bandwidth savings are assessed for various tunnel structures with different path layouts and load balancing strategies which are important traffic engineering characteristics in today's transport networks. We first give an overview of the options for tunnel implementations. Then we evaluate the bandwidth savings achieved with ABA for one of the following alternatives: shortest past first (SPF) tunnels, equal-cost multi-path (ECMP) tunnels, relaxed ECMP (xECMP) tunnels, and self-protecting multi-path (SPM) tunnels with either equal (kSPMe) or reciprocal (kSPMr) load distribution. The bandwidth savings are quantified for an example wide area network (WAN) using the LCA and LPCA traffic demand models derived in Section 4.4. Some of the results are published in [199].

4.5.1 Options for Tunnel Implementations

A tunnel between an ingress and an egress node is most simply implemented as a single path according to, e.g. the shortest path first (SPF) principle. An ECMP-based tunnel consists of an equal cost multi-path (ECMP) as defined in [25]. xECMP tunnels represent a kind of relaxed ECMP tunnels, i.e., all partial paths not longer than x times the shortest possible path are joined in the xECMP tunnel structure. This tunnel implementation may be reasonable for networks where only few equal cost paths between routers exist. From the concept of self-protecting multi-paths (SPMs) [200], the kSPMe and kSPMr tunnel implementations are derived. According to parameter k, a kSPM tunnel consists of the k link- and node-disjoint shortest paths [201, 202] between tunnel in- and egress nodes. These k shortest paths may certainly have different lengths. For a kSPMe tunnel, its traffic load is distributed equally among all k partial paths. For a kSPMr tunnel, the traffic load is distributed reciprocally to the partial path lengths, i.e., shorter partial paths carry larger traffic load shares than longer partial paths.

The performance measures in our study are the overall required network capacity $C_{X,Y}^Z$ and the bandwidth savings $\mathcal{B}_{X,Y}$ achievable with ABA compared to SBA. We calculate these measures for different capacity tunnel implementations $X \in \{SPF, ECMP, xECMP, kSPMe, kSPMr\}$, traffic demands models $Y \in \{LCA, LPCA\}$ (cf. Section 4.4.3), and BA methods $Z \in \{SBA, ABA\}$. All numerical results are computed for a target aggregate blocking probability $p_b = 10^{-3}$ and the request size distribution $\mathcal{R}_1$ (cf. Section 4.3.1).

4.5.2 SPF and ECMP Tunnel Implementation

Tables 4.4 and 4.5 show the overall required network capacities $C_{X,Y}^Z$ and the bandwidth savings $\mathcal{B}_{X,Y}$ achievable with ABA for the SPF and ECMP tunnel implementation, respectively. The results are calculated for different offered loads a_{b2b} and presented in tabular form because the differences between SPF and ECMP tunnel implementation are rather small. Both, the required network capacities and the bandwidth savings, increase with increasing offered load. For values $a_{b2b} \leq 10^4$, the capacities $C_{X,Y}^Z$ scale sub-proportionally with the offered load which is due to the superior economy of scale of larger links. For values $a_{b2b} \geq 10^4$, the achievable multiplexing gain diminishes and all capacities $C_{X,Y}^Z$ scale almost linearly with a_{b2b}. This holds for SPF as well as for ECMP tunnels. Likewise, the bandwidth savings $\mathcal{B}_{X,Y}$ first increase over-proportionally with the offered load and then converge slowly to a certain maximum that depends primarily on the demand model but also on the tunnel implementation. With the LCA model, only few bandwidth savings ($\approx 2 - 2.6\%$) are achievable. There is almost no difference between SPF and ECMP tunnel implementation. For the LPCA model, the bandwidth savings differ a little more and converge to $\mathcal{B}_{SPF,LPCA} \approx 17.8\%$ for SPF tunnels and $\mathcal{B}_{ECMP,LPCA} \approx 20\%$ for ECMP tunnels. Hence, ECMP tunnels are slightly more effective in connection with ABA than SPF tunnels. Please note that the values for $C_{SPF,Y}^{SBA}$ and $C_{ECMP,Y}^{SBA}$ in

a_{b2b}	$\mathcal{B}_{X,LCA}$	$\mathcal{C}^{SBA}_{X,LCA}$	$\mathcal{C}^{ABA}_{X,LCA}$	$\mathcal{B}_{X,LPCA}$	$\mathcal{C}^{SBA}_{X,LPCA}$	$\mathcal{C}^{ABA}_{X,LPCA}$
1E+01	1.06%	1.89E+07	1.87E+07	9.69%	1.85E+07	1.67E+07
1E+02	1.77%	7.07E+07	6.94E+07	14.47%	6.78E+07	5.80E+07
1E+03	2.11%	4.68E+08	4.58E+08	16.82%	4.44E+08	3.69E+08
1E+04	2.22%	4.10E+09	4.01E+09	17.54%	3.88E+09	3.20E+09
1E+05	2.25%	3.96E+10	3.87E+10	17.73%	3.74E+10	3.08E+10
1E+06	2.25%	3.92E+11	3.83E+11	17.79%	3.71E+11	3.05E+11

Table 4.4: *Network capacity requirements and bandwidth savings for SPF tunnels and different WAN traffic demand models ($X = SPF$).*

a_{b2b}	$\mathcal{B}_{X,LCA}$	$\mathcal{C}^{SBA}_{X,LCA}$	$\mathcal{C}^{ABA}_{X,LCA}$	$\mathcal{B}_{X,LPCA}$	$\mathcal{C}^{SBA}_{X,LPCA}$	$\mathcal{C}^{ABA}_{X,LPCA}$
1E+01	1.23%	1.89E+07	1.87E+07	11.00%	1.85E+07	1.64E+07
1E+02	1.98%	7.07E+07	6.93E+07	16.39%	6.78E+07	5.67E+07
1E+03	2.37%	4.68E+08	4.57E+08	19.00%	4.44E+08	3.60E+08
1E+04	2.50%	4.10E+09	4.00E+09	19.77%	3.88E+09	3.12E+09
1E+05	2.54%	3.96E+10	3.86E+10	19.97%	3.74E+10	2.99E+10
1E+06	2.55%	3.92E+11	3.82E+11	20.03%	3.71E+11	2.96E+11

Table 4.5: *Network capacity requirements and bandwidth savings for ECMP tunnels and different traffic demand models ($X = ECMP$).*

Tables 4.4 and 4.5 are identical per definition. In contrast, less overall network capacity is required for ECMP compared to SPF tunnels if ABA is used instead of SBA, i.e. $\forall a_{b2b} > 0 : \mathcal{C}^{ABA}_{ECMP,Y} < \mathcal{C}^{ABA}_{SPF,Y}$. If the tunnels are implemented according to ECMP, the network links need on average less capacity than for SPF tunnels which is explained by the composition of the traffic carried on these links. For SPF tunnels, we have on average 15 integral aggregates carried on a link, whereas for ECMP tunnels, we have on average 28 partial aggregates. A larger number of flows on a link increases the potential of capacity sharing for aggregates which have their busy hours at different times. This savings potential can only be exploited by ABA and not by SBA.

4.5.3 xECMP Tunnel Implementation

Multi-path tunnels exploit the potential of capacity sharing for aggregates to a larger degree than single path tunnels. However, the strict compliance with the equal cost constraint for partial paths in ECMP tunnels yields rather narrow multi-paths since the number of shortest paths of exactly the same length may be very limited in a network. As a consequence, the distribution of an aggregate among the partial paths of a strict ECMP tunnel is constrained by the width of that path. The width of an ECMP tunnel can be enlarged if the strict equal cost constraint is relaxed. This leads to xECMP tunnels which are constrained by relaxation parameter x, i.e., they subsume all partial paths not longer than x times the shortest possible path in their tunnel structure. Since parameter x is critical to the packet delay experienced in the network, the values of x are restricted to $x \in [1.0, 2.0]$ regarding a hop-count metric. For values $x > 1.0$, xECMP tunnels must be configured carefully in the network to avoid routing loops.

Figures 4.13(a) and 4.13(b) show the required network capacities $C_{xECMP,Y}^Z$ and the bandwidth savings $\mathcal{B}_{xECMP,Y}$ achievable with xECMP tunnels for different values of the relaxation parameter x. The results are computed for the request size distribution $\mathcal{R}_1$ and a blocking probability $p_b = 10^{-3}$ and they are illustrated for the LCA and LPCA traffic demand model in separated subfigures. The offered load is set to a constant value of $a_{b2b} = 10^4$ Erl. From previous investigations (cf. Section 4.4.3) we know that the multiplexing gain for an offered load $a_{b2b} \geq 10^4$ is widely exploited and, therefore, does not influence the illustrated results. Increasing relaxation parameter x from 1.0 to 1.2 and from 1.8 to 2.0 has no impact on $C_{xECMP,Y}^Z$ and $\mathcal{B}_{xECMP,Y}$ because the structures of the xECMP tunnels do not change for these transitions of x. In contrast, the required capacities and the bandwidth savings rise continuously for values x increasing from 1.2 to 1.8. The reason for the growing capacity requirements is the increased average path length in the xECMP tunnels that is due to the widening of the multi-path. From $x = 1.2$ to $x = 1.8$, the average number of links per xECMP tunnel rises from 4 to 30.

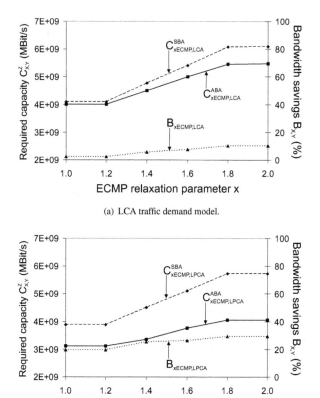

(a) LCA traffic demand model.

(b) LPCA traffic demand model.

Figure 4.13: *Network capacity requirements and bandwidth savings for extended equal cost multi-path tunnels (xECMP).*

Simultaneously, the average number of partial aggregates compiled on a single link rises from 28.1 to 182.9. Intensifying the load distribution causes that the network capacity requirements for ABA increase on average less with rising value x than those for SBA, i.e., $C_{xECMP,Y}^{SBA}$ increases stronger than $C_{xECMP,Y}^{ABA}$. As a consequence, the bandwidth savings $\mathcal{B}_{xECMP,LCA}$ increase from about 2.5% for $x \leq 1.2$ to 10.2% for $x \geq 1.8$ (cf. Figure 4.13(a)). In this domain of parameter x, the bandwidth savings $\mathcal{B}_{xECMP,LPCA}$ grow from about 20% to 30% (cf. Figure 4.13(b)).

4.5.4 kSPM Tunnel Implementation

The self-protecting multi-path (SPM) [200] is a multi-path protection switching mechanism that may be implemented, e.g., in MPLS networks. A capacity tunnel based on a kSPM consists of k link- and node-disjoint parallel paths that carry the traffic in normal operation mode and during local outages. If a partial path is affected by a network failure, the traffic is just distributed to the remaining $k-1$ companion paths. Constrained by the network topology, parameter k allows to control the width of a SPM. The SPM tunnel structure implements a simple and loop-free multi-path concept and, therefore, it is easier to configure than xECMP tunnels. From the SPM concept, we merely use the resource-disjoint multi-path structure for the capacity tunnels to asses their impact on the bandwidth savings achievable with ABA.

Figures 4.14(a) and 4.14(b) show the required network capacities $C_{kSPMe,Y}^{Z}$ and the bandwidth savings $\mathcal{B}_{kSPMe,Y}$ for different numbers of partial paths k per SPM tunnel with equal load distribution. Figures 4.15(a) and 4.15(b) show the corresponding results $C_{kSPMr,Y}^{Z}$ and $\mathcal{B}_{kSPMr,Y}$ for kSPM tunnels with a load distribution reciprocal to the partial path length. All results are calculated for the request size distribution $\mathcal{R}_1$ and a blocking probability $p_b = 10^{-3}$ and they are illustrated for the LCA and LPCA traffic demand model in separated subfigures. Like for the evaluation of xECMP tunnels, the offered load is set to $a_{b2b} = 10^4$ Erl and thus large enough to blind out the influence of the economy of scale.

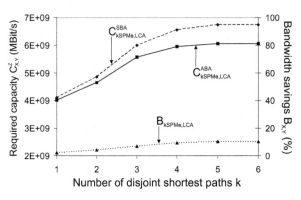

(a) LCA traffic demand model.

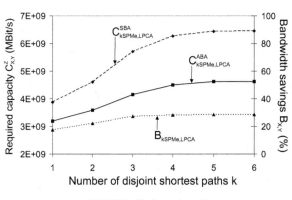

(b) LPCA traffic demand model.

Figure 4.14: *Network capacity requirements and bandwidth savings for self-protecting multi-paths with equal load balancing (kSPMe).*

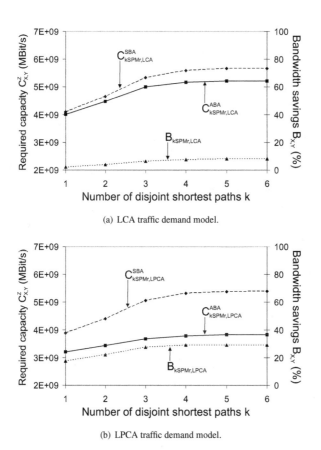

(a) LCA traffic demand model.

(b) LPCA traffic demand model.

Figure 4.15: *Network capacity requirements and bandwidth savings for self-protecting multi-paths with reciprocal load balancing (kSPMr).*

The network capacities $C^Z_{kSPMe,Y}$ and $C^Z_{kSPMr,Y}$ grow strongly for a maximum of $k \leq 4$ partial paths per SPM tunnel and they do it irrespectively of the load distribution option and the BA method. The capacity increase is due to the rising average path length of partial paths in the SPM tunnel. From $k = 2$ to $k = 6$, the average path length increases from 3.2 to 4.0, the average number of links per SPM tunnel increases from 6.4 to 13.2 and, simultaneously, the average number of partial aggregates per link rises from 37.7 to 77.9. For $k > 4$, the required network capacities $C^Z_{kSPMe,Y}$ and $C^Z_{kSPMr,Y}$ grow less. The reason is that only few ingress/egress node pairs exist for which more than 4 link- and node-disjoint paths can be provided in our test network. Although kSPMr tunnels require less overall network capacity than kSPMe tunnels, i.e. $\forall k > 1 : C^Z_{kSPMr,Y} < C^Z_{kSPMe,Y}$, the bandwidth savings for both implementations $X \in \{kSPMe, kSPMr\}$ are almost identical and range from $\mathcal{B}_{X,LCA} \approx 4.2\%$ for $k = 2$ to $\mathcal{B}_{X,LCA} \approx 10.2\%$ for $k = 6$ regarding the LCA traffic demand model. For these values of k, the LPCA model yields bandwidth savings ranging from $\mathcal{B}_{X,LPCA} \approx 17.5\%$ to $\mathcal{B}_{X,LPCA} \approx 29\%$.

Summary

We have illustrated the impact of different tunnel implementations on the bandwidth savings achievable with ABA. The bandwidth savings potential is investigated for an example wide area network (WAN) using two different WAN traffic demand models derived in the previous section. Five different tunnel implementations are considered: single path tunnels according to the shortest path first (SPF) principle, equal cost multi-path (ECMP) tunnels, relaxed ECMP (xECMP) tunnels, and self-protecting multi-path (SPM) tunnels with equal (kSPMe) or reciprocal (kSPMr) load distribution among the k partial paths.

Our analytical results show that the bandwidth savings potential of ABA depends primariliy on the traffic demand model but also on the tunnel implementation. For the LCA model, the bandwidth savings range from about 2.2% for SPF tunnels, 2.5% for ECMP tunnels, 5.8% for xECMP tunnels with relaxation parameter $x = 1.4$, to 8.5% for kSPMe and kSPMr tunnels with $k = 4$ partial paths per tunnel. For the LPCA model, about 17.5% capacity savings were achievable with SPF tunnels, 20% with ECMP tunnels, 25.5% with xECMP tunnels setting $x = 1.4$, and about 28.5% for kSPMe and kSPMr tunnels setting $k = 4$. All results are computed for a b2b blocking probabilty $p_b = 10^{-3}$, an average b2b offered load $a_{b2b} = 10^4$, and the request size distribution $\mathcal{R}_1$. These values are of course specific to the example test network and the assumed traffic demand models. However, these conditions apply for all investigated tunnel implementations. Hence, the analytical results advocate multi-path tunnels which are also favorable if network resilience is taken into account. Corresponding aspects are considered in the next section.

4.6 Impact of Resilience Requirements on ABA Bandwidth Savings

The fault tolerance of a network regarding local outages is called resilience. Hence, a network is resilient if traffic flows reach their destination despite of occuring network failures that may affect the physical infrastructure or just disrupt communication paths [203]. In traditional telephone systems, most vital systems have redundant layouts. To improve the resilience of general connection-oriented networks, the reliability of the switching nodes must be increased and backup communication lines must be provided. Alternatively, backup connections for individual flows can be set up over disjoint paths to provide hot standbys but this is a considerable overhead. In any case, 100% extra capacity must be provided. Using the connectionless IP technology, traffic can simply be deviated around a failure location by adapting the routing to the modified network topology. Since tranmission capacity is not exclusively dedicated to specific connections, extra capacity deployed in the network can be shared by different flows in different outage scenarios. However, care must be taken that enough capacity is provided along the detours to prevent congestion. Link overload probabilities may be calculated which help to decide on potential infrastructure upgrades [204, 205].

Investigating the impact of resilience requirements on the bandwidth savings potential of ABA is computationally expensive. Even if the set of considered network failures is restricted to only single failures of links and routers, the number of necessary calculations is rather large. Our test network in Figure 4.9, for instance, consists of 26 nodes and 55 bidirectional links which results in $26+55+1=82$ failure scenarios that must be considered. For SBA this means that the network dimensioning approach described in Section 4.3.2 must be performed 82 times. If we reoptimize the tunnel sizes every 5 minutes a day for ABA, the network must be dimensioned even $82 \cdot 288 = 23616$ times. For the ease of completeness, these calulations are performed once for a 3SPMr tunnel implementation, setting $a_{b2b} = 10^4$, $p_b = 10^{-3}$ and $\mathcal{R}_1$ as usual. Our results show that the bandwidth savings with and without resilience requirements differ only little. The bandwidth savings slightly decrease from 6.32% without resilience to 5.21% with resilience for the LCA traffic demand model, and from 27.60% to 26.19% for the LPCA model. This slight decrease of the bandwidth savings is due to the extra capacity that is bound in the statically allocated tunnels. This capacity is often unused at secondary times and can thus be used efficiently for backup purposes. In contrast, the capacity allocated in adaptive tunnels is always as small as possible which decreases the potential for capacity sharing in case of network outage.

5 Conclusion

This work is driven by the technical and economical need for resource-efficient QoS provisioning in *next generation networks* (NGNs). NGNs dissolve the current coexistence of circuit-switched voice networks and packet-switched data networks. They use IP technology, provide high reliability, and offer QoS-guaranteed services with a resource efficiency much higher than in today's overprovisioned Internet backbones. Instead of mere *capacity overprovisioning* (CO) they rely on *admission control* (AC) mechanisms which limit the traffic admitted to individual links or to networks to achieve real-time QoS in terms of packet loss and delay. Strict QoS requirements can only be fulfilled by AC since CO is unable to protect the available resources from overutilization due to unpredictable traffic changes.

Therefore, the content of this work concerns AC systems and associated bandwidth allocation strategies. There are two major contributions: (1) a new link-oriented AC approach called *experience-based admission control* (EBAC) which simultaneously aims at high resource efficiency while maintaining QoS and (2) *adaptive bandwidth allocation* (ABA) for admission-controlled capacity tunnels which enables bandwidth savings and thus reduces the CAPEX for network infrastructure.

The new EBAC concept addresses the weaknesses of conventional AC methods, i.e., the poor resource utilization of parameter-based AC and the susceptibility to QoS violations of measurement-based AC. To overcome these problems, EBAC overbooks the capacity of a single link by a safely calculated overbooking factor. Its design includes the implementation of the EBAC admission decision, the calculation of a safe overbooking factor based on the experience of the EBAC system, and the definition of the memory of EBAC from which it gains experience. The length of this memory is adjustable by its half-life period, i.e., the time after which the collected experience looses half of its importance for the overbooking factor calculation. The half-life period strongly influences the adaptation speed of the overbooking factor to changing traffic conditions on the link. Therefore, the performance of EBAC is investigated by simulations for different memory settings and under various traffic conditions. The traffic controlled by EBAC is modeled on two levels, i.e. the flow scale level and the packet scale level.

For static traffic, EBAC reaches steady state and its performance is measured by the achieved overbooking factor and the resulting packet delay. The corresponding simulations give a proof of concept, allow for recommendations concerning the EBAC system parameters, and prove the robustness of EBAC against traffic variability. Moreover, if EBAC is applied to larger links, it increases the overbooking factor and thus takes advantage of economy of scale.

For changing traffic, EBAC shows its transient behavior and its performance is measured by the link utilization and the system response time, i.e., the time required by EBAC to adapt the overbooking factor to current traffic conditions. The corresponding simulation results strongly depend on the EBAC memory. Sudden changes of the packet level traffic characteristics are simulated as worst case scenarios to obtain upper bounds on the EBAC response time. For a suddenly decreasing traffic intensity, the QoS of admitted traffic is not at risk and the response time depends linearly on the half-life period of the memory. However, for a suddenly increasing traffic intensity, the QoS is temporarily compromised and the overall EBAC response time is split into QoS restoration time and utilization restoration time. While the latter depends again linearly on the half-life period, the time required to restore QoS is independent thereof.

EBAC with *type-specific overbooking* (TSOB) extends the conventional EBAC system to account for different traffic types. This extension improves the EBAC performance with regard to traffic changes on the flow scale level. For static traffic, EBAC with TSOB safely increases the link utilization. For a decreasing traffic intensity due to changes in the traffic mix, it adapts the overbooking factor much faster than conventional EBAC which leads to a higher and more stable link utilization during transient phases. For a comparable increasing traffic intensity, EBAC with TSOB avoids overload situations where conventional EBAC fails.

Despite the link-oriented design of EBAC, this new approach is well applicable in a network-wide scope without the need for a tedious link-by-link application. To reach that goal, EBAC may be applied to virtual *border-to-border* (b2b) capacity tunnels. The *(generalized) multi-protocol label switching* ((G)MPLS) technology, for instance, provides all necessary means for the implementation of such tunnels by label switched paths.

Adaptive bandwidth allocation for admission-controlled capacity tunnels enhances the idea of *network AC* (NAC) based on tunnels between pairs of network border routers. Using ABA to adapt the tunnel sizes enables bandwidth savings compared to *static bandwidth allocation* (SBA). The concept of ABA for capacity tunnels fits in the context of efficient *network resource management* (NRM). Its performance is evaluated analytically by a new network dimensioning approach which differs fundamentally from the conventional methods often used in the context of call blocking analysis in ATM networks. Instead of abstract blocking probabilities, this approach yields more meaningful results in terms of bandwidth savings that are influenced by many network characteristics.

Traffic demand models have a signifcant impact on the bandwidth savings. For variable b2b traffic aggregates that oscillate opportunistically on all network links, the maximum bandwidth savings of 50% are achieved only if the offered load in the network is high enough. More realistic traffic demand models constructed proportionally to the user activities at the nodes of a *wide area network* (WAN) can be categorized into *linearity to provider activity* (LPA), *linearity to consumer activity* (LCA), and *linearity to provider and consumer activity* (LPCA). Using simple single path tunnels, bandwidth savings are hardly achievable if the LPA/LCA model ($\approx 2.2\%$) is assumed. More significant savings are obtained in case of the LPCA model ($\approx 17.5\%$). The analysis of the time-dependent capacity requirements of a single link reveals that the bandwidth savings significantly depend on the overlapping of busy hours of aggregates routed over that link. The savings increase if these busy periods occur at different times.

Tunnel implementations have a major impact on the overall required network capacity but also on the bandwidth savings. To illustrate this influence, we distinguish between single path tunnels according to the *shortest path first* (SPF) principle, *equal cost multi-path* (ECMP) tunnels, relaxed ECMP (xECMP) tunnels, and *self-protecting multi-path* (SPM) tunnels with equal (kSPMe) or reciprocal (kSPMr) load distribution, and assume the previously identified WAN traffic demand models. SPF tunnels perform worst and save the least bandwidth for LPA/LCA ($\approx 2.2\%$) and LPCA ($\approx 17.5\%$). Among the multi-path tunnels, the kSPM implementations perform best and save the most bandwidth for LPA/LCA ($\approx 8.5\%$) and LPCA ($\approx 28.5\%$). Although specific to our test network, these values advocate multi-path tunnels which are also favorable with regard to network resilience. However, the bandwidth savings achievable with ABA slightly decrease ($\approx 1\%$) if network resilience is taken into account. This is reasonable since the capacity assigned to adaptive tunnels is always as small as possible which decreases the potential for capacity sharing in case of network failures.

In conclusion, the resources in NGNs must be exclusively dedicated to admitted traffic to guarantee QoS. For that purpose, robust and efficient concepts for NRM are required to control the requested bandwidth with regard to the available transmission capacity. Sophisticated AC will be a key function for NRM in NGNs and, therefore, efficient resource management concepts like experience-based admission control and adaptive bandwidth allocation for admission-controlled capacity tunnels, as presented in this work are appealing for NGN solutions.

List of Abbreviations

CCITT	Comité Consultatif International Télégraphique et Télé-phonique, page 118
CIDR	classless inter-domain routing, page 20
CLI	command line interface, page 116
CO	capacity overprovisioning, page 1
CR-LDP	constraint-based label distribution protocol, page 27
CS	complete sharing, page 135
CSMA/CD	carrier sense multiple access with collision detection, page 9
CSPF	constrained shortest path first, page 124
DHT	distributed hash table, page 14
DiffServ	differentiated services, page 32
DNS	domain name system, page 14
DSCP	differentiated services code point, page 32
E-BGP	exterior border gateway protocol, page 25
e2e	end-to-end, page 2
EBAC	experience-based admission control, page 39
ECMP	equal cost multi-path, page 24
EDF	earliest deadline first, page 33
EGP	exterior gateway protocol, page 22
Erl	Erlang, page 133

EWMA	exponentially-weighted moving average, page 99
FEC	forwarding equivalent class, page 124
FIFO	first-in-first-out, page 33
FTP	file transfer protocol, page 14
FWP	framework program, page 37
GMPLS	generalized multi-protocol label switching, page 28
GPL	GNU public license, page 14
GPS	generalized processor sharing, page 33
HDLC	high-level data link control, page 9
HTTP	hypertext transfer protocol, page 8
I-BGP	interior border gateway protocol, page 25
IB/EB-NAC	ingress and egress budget-based network admission control, page 48
ICANN	Internet Corporation for Assigned Names and Numbers, page 18
ICMP	Internet control message protocol, page 11
IETF	Internet Engineering Task Force, page 8
IGP	interior gateway protocol, page 22
ILB/ELB-NAC	ingress link budget- and egress link budget-based network admission control, page 49
ILM	incoming label map, page 26

IP-FRR	Internet protocol fast reroute, page 31
IPTV	Internet protocol television, page 16
IPv4	Internet protocol version 4, page 12
IPv6	Internet protocol version 6, page 12
IS-IS	intermediate system to intermediate system, page 24
ISO	International Standardization Organization, page 10
ISP	Internet service provider, page 2
IST	information society technologies, page 37
ITU	International Telecommunication Union, page 17
IXP	Internet exchange point, page 19
KING	key components for the Internet of the next generation, page 38
LAC	link admission control, page 44
LB-NAC	link budget-based network admission control, page 48
LDP	label distribution protocol, page 27
LER	label edge router, page 26
LL	link layer, page 9
LLC	logical link control, page 9
LMP	link management protocol, page 29
LSA	link state advertisement, page 24

SIP	session initiation protocol, page 16
SLA	service level agreement, page 32
SMTP	simple mail transfer protocol, page 14
SP	static priority, page 33
TCP	transmission control protocol, page 13
TE	traffic engineering, page 27
TEWMA	time exponentially-weighted moving average, page 59
TEWMH	time exponentially-weighted moving histogram, page 58
TL	transport layer, page 8
ToS	type of service, page 11
TR	trunk reservation, page 135
TTL	time-to-live, page 11
UDP	user datagram protocol, page 13
URL	uniform resource locator, page 8
VoD	video on demand, page 16
VoIP	voice over Internet protocol, page 37
VPN	virtual private network, page 30
WFQ	weighted fair queuing, page 33
WRR	weighted round robin, page 33
WWW	worldwide web, page 14

5 Conclusion

List of Figures

List of Figures

Bibliography

[1] J. Postel, "RFC 791: Internet Protocol," August 1981.

[2] S. Deering and R. Hinden, "RFC 2460: Internet Protocol Version 6 (IPv6) Specification," December 1998.

[3] "Internet Engineering Task Force (IETF)." http://www.ietf.org/.

[4] J. Postel, "RFC 793: Transmission Control Protocol," September 1981.

[5] Institute of Electrical and Electronics Engineers, "Carrier Sense Multiple Access with Collision Detection (CSMA/CD) Access Method and Physical Layer Specifications." ANSI/IEEE Std 802.3, 1985.

[6] L. L. Peterson and B. S. Davie, *Computer Networks: A Systems Approach.* Morgan and Kaufman, 1996.

[7] N. Vicari, *Modeling of Internet Traffic: Internet Access Influence, User Interference, and TCP Behavior.* PhD thesis, University of Würzburg, April 2003.

[8] J. Postel, "RFC 768: User Datagram Protocol," September 1980.

[9] S. Sen and J. Wang, "Analyzing Peer-to-Peer Traffic Across Large Networks," *IEEE/ACM Transactions on Networking*, vol. 12, pp. 219–232, April 2004.

[10] R. Steinmetz and K. Wehrle, *Peer-to-Peer Systems and Applications.* Springer, October 2005.

[11] H. Schulzrinne, S. Casner, R. Frederick, and V. Jacobson, "RFC 3550: RTP - A Transport Protocol for Real-Time Applications," July 2003.

[12] H. Schulzrinne, A. Rao, and R. Lanphier, "RFC 2326: Real Time Streaming Protocol (RTSP)," April 1998.

[13] J. Rosenberg, H. Schulzrinne, *et al.*, "RFC 3261: SIP: Session Initiation Protocol," June 2002.

[14] "International Telecommunication Union (ITU)." http://www.itu.int/.

[15] J. Postel, "RFC 792: Internet Control Message Protocol," September 1981.

[16] R. Braden *et al.*, "RFC 2205: Resource ReSerVation Protocol (RSVP) – Version 1 Functional Specification," September 1997.

[17] J. F. Kurose and K. W. Ross, *Computer Networking*. Addison Wesley, May 2004.

[18] N. Spring, R. Mahajan, D. Wetherall, and T. Anderson, "Measuring ISP Topologies with Rocketfuel," *IEEE/ACM Transactions on Networking*, vol. 12, pp. 2–16, February 2004.

[19] "Internet Corporation For Assigned Names and Numbers (ICANN)." http://www.icann.org/.

[20] K. Xu, Z. Duan, Z.-L. Zhang, and J. Chandrashekar, "On Properties of Internet Exchange Points and Their Impact on AS Topology and Relationship," in *Proc. of IFIP-TC6 Networking Conference (NETWORKING)*, pp. 284–295, May 2004.

[21] C. Huitema, *Routing on the Internet*. Prentice Hall, November 1999.

[22] L. R. Ford and D. R. Fulkerson, *Flows in Networks*. Princeton University Press, 1962.

[23] G. Malking, "RFC 2453: Routing Information Protocol (RIP) Version 2," November 1998.

[24] E. W. Dijkstra, "A Note on Two Problems in Connexion with Graphs," *Numerische Mathematik*, vol. 1, pp. 269–271, 1959.

[25] J. Moy, "RFC 2328: OSPF Version 2," April 1998.

[26] D. Oran, "RFC 1142: OSI IS-IS Intra-domain Routing Protocol," February 1990.

[27] Y. Rekhter and T. Li, "RFC 1771: A Border Gateway Protocol Version 4 (BGP-4)," March 1995.

[28] L. Andersson, P. Doolan, N. Feldman, A. Fredette, and B. Thomas, "RFC 3036: LDP Specification," January 2001.

[29] D. O. Awduche, L. Berger, D.-H. Gan, T. Li, V. Srinivasan, and G. Swallow, "RFC 3209: RSVP-TE: Extensions to RSVP for LSP Tunnels," December 2001.

[30] B. Jamoussi *et al.*, "RFC 3212: Constraint-Based LSP Setup using LDP," January 2002.

[31] E. Rosen, A. Viswanathan, and R. Callon, "RFC 3031: Multiprotocol Label Switching Architecture," January 2001.

[32] J. Wroclawski, "RFC 2210: The Use of RSVP with IETF Integrated Services," September 1997.

[33] B. Braden, D. Clark, and S. Shenker, "RFC 1633: Integrated Services in the Internet Architecture: an Overview," June 1994.

[34] G. Swallow, "MPLS Advantages for Traffic Engineering," *IEEE Communications Magazine*, vol. 37, pp. 54–57, December 1999.

[35] D. O. Awduche, "MPLS and Traffic Engineering in IP Networks," *IEEE Communications Magazine*, vol. 37, pp. 42–47, December 1999.

[36] X. Xiao, A. Hannan, and L. M. Ni, "Traffic Engineering with MPLS in the Internet," *IEEE Network Magazine*, vol. 38, pp. 28–33, March/April 2000.

[37] M. Menth, A. Reifert, and J. Milbrandt, "CSPF-Routed and Traffic-Driven Construction of LSP Hierarchies," in *Proc. of Architectures for Quality of Service in the Internet (Art-QoS)*, March 2003.

[38] E. Mannie, "RFC 3945: Generalized Multi-Protocol Label Switching (GMPLS) Architecture," October 2004.

[39] IETF Working Group on, "Common Control and Measurement Plane (CCAMP)." http://www.ietf.org/html.charters/ccamp-charter.html.

[40] A. Banerjee, J. Drake, J. P. Lang, B. Turner, K. Kompella, and Y. Rekhter, "Generalized Multiprotocol Label Switching: An Overview of Routing and Management Enhancements," *IEEE Communications Magazine*, vol. 39, pp. 144–150, January 2001.

[41] A. Banerjee, J. Drake, J. Lang, B. Turner, D. Awduche, L. Berger, K. Kompella, and Y. Rekhter, "Generalized Multiprotocol Label Switching: An Overview of Signaling Enhancements and Recovery Techniques," *IEEE Communications Magazine*, vol. 39, pp. 144–151, July 2001.

[42] A. Farrel and I. Bryskin, *GMPLS. Architecture and Applications*. Morgan Kaufmann, January 2006.

[43] L. Andersson *et al.*, "RFC 4206: Label Switched Paths (LSP) Hierarchy with Generalized Multi-Protocol Label Switching (GMPLS) Traffic Engineering (TE)," October 2005.

[44] J. Lang, "RFC 4204: Link Management Protocol (LMP)," October 2005.

[45] S. Floyd and V. Jacobson, "Link-Sharing and Resource Management Models for Packet Networks," *IEEE/ACM Transactions on Networking*, vol. 3, pp. 365–386, August 1995.

[46] M. Shand and S. Bryant, "I-D: IP Fast Reroute Framework," March 2006.

[47] P. Pan, G. Swallow, and A. Atlas, "RFC 4090: Fast Reroute Extensions to RSVP-TE for LSP Tunnels," May 2005.

[48] S. Blake *et al.*, "RFC 2475: An Architecture for Differentiated Services," December 1998.

[49] M. May, J.-C. Bolot, A. Jean-Marie, and C. Diot, "Simple Performance Models of Differentiated Services Schemes for the Internet," in *Proc. of IEEE Conference on Computer Communications (INFOCOM)*, April 1999.

[50] S. Floyd and V. Jacobson, "Random Early Detection Gateways for Congestion Avoidance," *IEEE/ACM Transactions on Networking*, vol. 1, pp. 397–413, August 1993.

[51] K. Kumaran, G. Margrave, D. Mitra, and K. R. Stanley, "Novel Techniques for Design and Control of Generalized Processor Sharing Schedulers for Multiple QoS Classes," in *Proc. of IEEE Conference on Computer Communications (INFOCOM)*, pp. 932–941, March 2000.

[52] A. Demers, S. Keshav, and S. Shenker, "Analysis and Simulation of a Fair Queuing Algorithm," in *Proc. of ACM Special Interest Group on Data Communications (SIGCOMM)*, pp. 3–12, August 1989.

[53] E. L. Hahne, "Round Robin Scheduling for Max-Min Fairness in Data Networks," *IEEE Journal on Selected Areas in Communications*, vol. 9, pp. 1024–1039, September 1991.

[54] M. Andrews, "Probabilistic End-to-End Delay Bounds for Earliest Deadline First Scheduling," in *Proc. of IEEE Conference on Computer Communications (INFOCOM)*, March 2000.

[55] C. Fraleigh, F. Tobabi, and C. Diot, "Provisioning IP Backbone Networks to Support Latency Sensitive Traffic," in *Proc. of IEEE Conference on Computer Communications (INFOCOM)*, April 2003.

[56] K. Papagiannaki, N. Taft, Z.-L. Zhang, and C. Diot, "Long-Term Forecasting of Internet Backbone Traffic: Observations and Initial Models," in *Proc. of IEEE Conference on Computer Communications (INFOCOM)*, April 2003.

[57] T. Schwabe and C. G. Gruber, "Traffic Variations Caused by Inter-Domain Re-Routing," in *Proc. of International Workshop on the Design of Reliable Communication Networks (DRCN)*, October 2005.

[58] A. Odlyzko, "Data Networks are Lightly Utilized, and will Stay that Way," *The Review of Network Economics*, vol. 2, pp. 210–237, September 2003.

[59] R. Martin, M. Menth, and J. Charzinski, "Comparison of Border-to-Border Budget Based Network Admission Control and Capacity Overprovisioning," in *Proc. of IFIP-TC6 Networking Conference (NETWORKING)*, pp. 1056–1068, May 2005.

[60] R. Martin, M. Menth, and J. Charzinski, "Comparison of Link-by-Link Admission Control and Capacity Overprovisioning," in *Proc. of International Teletraffic Congress (ITC)*, August 2005.

[61] M. Menth, J. Milbrandt, and F. Zeiger, "Elastic Token Bucket - A Traffic Characterization for Time-Limited Bursty Traffic," in *Proc. of GI/ITG Conference on Measuring, Modelling and Evaluation of Computer and Communication Systems (MMB) together with Polish-German Teletraffic Symposium (PGTS)*, pp. 325–334, September 2004.

[62] Y. Bernet *et al.*, "RFC 2998: A Framework for Integrated Services Operation over Diffserv Networks," November 2000.

[63] M. Menth, *Efficient Admission Control and Routing for Resilient Communication Networks*. PhD thesis, University of Würzburg, July 2004.

[64] M. N. Ellanti, S. S. Gorshe, L. G. Raman, and W. D. Grover, *Next Generation Transport Networks : Data, Management, and Control Planes*. Springer, April 2005.

[65] "Internet2." http://www.internet2.org/.

[66] "Traffic Engineering for Quality of Service in the Internet, at Large Scale (TEQUILA)." http://www.ist-tequila.org/.

[67] "Adaptive Resource Control for QoS Using an IP-based Layered Architecture (AQUILA)." http://www-st.inf.tu-dresden.de/aquila/.

[68] "An Open Platform for Developing, Deploying, and Accessing Planetary-Scale Services (PlanetLab)." https://www.planet-lab.org/.

[69] "Global Environment for Network Innovations (GENI)." http://www.geni.net/.

[70] "Efficient Integrated Backbone (EIBONE)." http://www.dlr.de/pt_it/kt/foerderbereiche/photonische_kommunikationsnetze/Eibone/.

[71] "Key Components for the Internet of the Next Generation (KING)." http://www.siemens.com/king.

[72] M. Naghshineh and M. Schwartz, "Distributed Call Admission Control in Mobile/Wireless Networks," *IEEE Journal on Selected Areas in Communications*, vol. 14, pp. 711–717, May 1996.

[73] S. Garg and M. Kappes, "Admission Control for VoIP Traffic in IEEE 802.11 Networks," in *Proc. of IEEE Global Telecommunications Conference (GLOBECOM)*, vol. 6, pp. 3514–3518, December 2003.

[74] D. Shen and C. Ji, "Admission of Multimedia Traffic for Third Generation CDMA Network," in *Proc. of IEEE Conference on Computer Communications (INFOCOM)*, pp. 1077–1086, March 2000.

[75] N. Muller, *IP Convergence: The Next Revolution in Telecommunications*. Artech House, January 2000.

[76] S. Jordan and P. P. Varaiya, "Control of Multiple Service, Multiple Resource Communication Networks," *IEEE Transactions on Communications*, vol. 42, pp. 2979–2988, November 1994.

[77] K. Lindberger, "Dimensioning and Design Methods for Integrated ATM Networks," in *Proc. of International Teletraffic Congress (ITC)*, June 1994.

[78] A. Elwalid, D. Mitra, and R. H. Wentworth, "A New Approach for Allocating Buffers and Bandwidth to Heterogeneous, Regulated Traffic in an ATM Node," *IEEE Journal on Selected Areas in Communications*, vol. 13, pp. 1115–1127, August 1995.

[79] F. Kelly, *Stochastic Networks: Theory and Applications*, ch. Notes on Effective Bandwidths, pp. 141–168. Oxford University Press, 1996.

[80] L. Kleinrock, *Queueing Systems*. John Wiley & Sons, 1975.

[81] D. Abendroth and U. Killat, "Intelligent Shaping: Well Shaped Throughout the Entire Network?," in *Proc. of IEEE Conference on Computer Communications (INFOCOM)*, June 2002.

[82] J. Roberts, U. Mocci, and J. Virtamo, *Broadband Network Teletraffic - Final Report of Action COST 242*. Springer, 1996.

[83] S. Shenker, C. Partridge, and R. Guerin, "RFC 2212: Specification of Guaranteed Quality of Service," September 1997.

[84] J. L. Boudec, "Application of Network Calculus to Guaranteed Service Networks," *IEEE Network Magazine*, vol. 44, May 1998.

[85] J. Wroclawski, "RFC 2211: Specification of the Controlled-Load Network Element Service," September 1997.

[86] M. Grossglauser and D. Tse, "A Framework for Robust Measurement-Based Admission Control," *IEEE/ACM Transactions on Networking*, vol. 7, pp. 293–309, June 1999.

[87] M. Grossglauser and D. Tse, "A Time-Scale Decomposition Approach to Measurement-Based Admission Control," *IEEE/ACM Transactions on Networking*, vol. 11, pp. 550–563, August 2003.

[88] S. Jamin, S. Shenker, and P. Danzig, "Comparison of Measurement-Based Call Admission Control Algorithms for Controlled-Load Service," in *Proc. of IEEE Conference on Computer Communications (INFOCOM)*, pp. 973–980, March 1997.

[89] Z. Turanyi, A. Veres, and A. Olah, "A Family of Measurement-Based Admission Control Algorithms," in *Proc. of IFIP Conference on Performance of Information and Communication Systems*, May 1998.

[90] L. Breslau, S. Jamin, and S. Shenker, "Comments on the Performance of Measurement-Based Admission Control Algorithms," in *Proc. of IEEE Conference on Computer Communications (INFOCOM)*, pp. 1233–1242, March 2000.

[91] K. Shiomoto, N. Yamanaka, and T. Takahashi, "Overview of Measurement-Based Connection Admission Control Methods in ATM Networks," *IEEE Communications Surveys & Tutorials*, vol. 2, pp. 2–13, January 1999.

[92] H. van den Berg and M. Mandjes, "Admission Control in Integrated Networks: Overview and Evaluation," in *Proc. of International Conference on Telecommunication Systems, Modeling and Analysis (ICTSM)*, pp. 132–151, 2000.

[93] J. Qiu and E. Knightly, "Measurement-Based Admission Control with Aggregate Traffic Envelopes," *IEEE/ACM Transactions on Networking*, vol. 9, pp. 199–210, April 2001.

[94] S. Georgoulas, P. Trimintzios, and G. Pavlou, "Joint Measurement- and Traffic Descriptor-based Admission Control at Real-Time Traffic Aggregation Points," in *Proc. of IEEE International Conference on Communications (ICC)*, June 2004.

[95] S. Jamin, P. Danzig, S. J. Shenker, and L. Zhang, "Measurement-Based Admission Control Algorithms for Controlled-Load Services Packet Networks," in *Proc. of ACM SIGCOMM Symposium on Communications Architectures & Protocols*, 1995.

[96] R. Gibbens and F. Kelly, "Measurement-Based Connection Admission Control," in *Proc. of International Teletraffic Congress (ITC)*, June 1997.

[97] T. Lee, M. Zukerman, and R. Addie, "Admission Control Schemes for Bursty Multimedia Traffic," in *Proc. of IEEE Conference on Computer Communications (INFOCOM)*, pp. 478–487, April 2001.

[98] M. Dabrowski and F. Strohmeier, "Measurement-Based Admission Control in AQUILA Network and Improvements by Passive Measurements," in *Proc. of Architectures for Quality of Service in the Internet (Art-QoS)*, March 2003.

[99] R. J. Gibbens and F. P. Kelly, "Distributed Connection Acceptance Control for a Connectionless Network," in *Proc. of International Teletraffic Congress (ITC)*, pp. 941–952, June 1999.

[100] C. Cetinkaya and E. Knightly, "Egress Admission Control," in *Proc. of IEEE Conference on Computer Communications (INFOCOM)*, pp. 1471–1480, March 2000.

[101] V. Elek, G. Karlsson, and R. Rönngren, "Admission Control Based on End-to-End Measurements," in *Proc. of IEEE Conference on Computer Communications (INFOCOM)*, pp. 1233–1242, March 2000.

[102] F. Kelly, P. Key, and S. Zachary, "Distributed Admission Control," *IEEE Journal on Selected Areas in Communications*, vol. 18, pp. 2617–2628, December 2000.

[103] L. Breslau, E. Knightly, S. Shenker, and H. Zhang, "Endpoint Admission Control: Architectural Issues and Performance," in *Proc. of ACM SIGCOMM Symposium on Communications Architectures & Protocols*, August 2000.

[104] I. Más and G. Karlsson, "PBAC: Probe-Based Admission Control," in *Proc. of International Workshop on Quality of future Internet Services (QofIS)*, September 2001.

[105] O. Hagsand, I. Más, I. Marsh, and G. Karlsson, "Self-Admission Control for IP Telephony Using Early Quality Estimation," in *Proc. of IFIP-TC6 Networking Conference (NETWORKING)*, pp. 381–391, May 2004.

[106] S. B. Fredj, S. Oueslati-Boulahia, and J. W. Roberts, "Measurement-Based Admission Control for Elastic Traffic," in *Proc. of International Teletraffic Congress (ITC)*, December 2001.

[107] N. G. Duffield, P. Goyal, A. G. Greenberg, P. P. Mishra, K. K. Ramakrishnan, and J. E. van der Merive, "A Flexible Model for Resource Management in Virtual Private Networks," in *Proc. of ACM Special Interest Group on Data Communications (SIGCOMM)*, pp. 95–108, August 1999.

[108] A. Riedl, T. Bauschert, and J. Frings, "On the Dimensioning of Voice over IP Networks for Various Call Admission Control Schemes," in *Proc. of International Teletraffic Congress (ITC)*, pp. 1311–1320, September 2003.

[109] T. Bauschert, *Optimale Dimensionierung von ATM-Weitverkehrsnetzen mit mehrstufiger Durchschaltung*. PhD thesis, Technical University of München, 1997.

[110] S. O. Larsson, "Comparisons of Different Approaches for Capacity Management in ATM Networks," in *Proc. of Conference on Local Computer Networks (LCN)*, pp. 462–471, November 2000.

[111] J. Kilpi and I. Norros, "Testing the Gaussian Approximation of Aggregate Traffic," in *Proc. of ACM SIGCOMM Internet Measurement Workshop*, November 2002.

[112] G. van Hoey, D. de Vleeschauwer, B. Steyaert, V. Ingelbrecht, and H. Brunel, "Benefit of Admission Control in Aggregation Network Dimensioning for Video Services," in *Proc. of IFIP-TC6 Networking Conference (NETWORKING)*, pp. 357–368, May 2004.

[113] J. Milbrandt, M. Menth, and S. Oechsner, "EBAC - A Simple Admission Control Mechanism," in *Proc. of IEEE International Conference on Network Protocols (ICNP)*, October 2004.

[114] M. Menth, J. Milbrandt, and S. Oechsner, "Experience Based Admission Control (EBAC)," in *Proc. of IEEE Symposium on Computers and Communications (ISCC)*, June 2004.

[115] M. Menth, J. Milbrandt, and J. Junker, "Time-Exponentially Weighted Moving Histograms (TEWMH) for Self-Adaptive Systems," in *Proc. of IEEE Global Telecommunications Conference (GLOBECOM)*, November 2006.

[116] R. Martin and M. Menth, "Improving the Timeliness of Rate Measurements," in *Proc. of GI/ITG Conference on Measuring, Modelling and Evaluation of Computer and Communication Systems (MMB) together with Polish-German Teletraffic Symposium (PGTS)*, September 2004.

[117] F. Hübner and P. Tran-Gia, "An Analysis of Multi-Service Systems with Trunk Reservation Mechanisms," Technical Report No. 40, University of Würzburg, Institute of Computer Science, April 1992.

[118] A. M. Law and W. D. Kelton, *Simulation Modeling and Analysis*. McGraw-Hill, 2000.

[119] V. Paxson and S. Floyd, "Wide-Area Traffic: The Failure of Poisson Modeling," *IEEE/ACM Transactions on Networking*, vol. 3, pp. 226–244, June 1995.

[120] P. Tran-Gia, *Einführung in die Leistungsbewertung und Verkehrstheorie*. Oldenbourg, Juli 2005.

[121] J. Milbrandt, M. Menth, and J. Junker, "Performance of Experience-Based Admission Control in the Presence of Traffic Changes," in *Proc. of IFIP-TC6 Networking Conference (NETWORKING)*, May 2006.

[122] J. Milbrandt, M. Menth, and J. Junker, "Experience-Based Admission Control with Type-Specific Overbooking," in *Proc. of IEEE International Workshop on IP Operations and Management (IPOM)*, October 2006.

[123] I. N. Bronstein *et al.*, *Taschenbuch der Mathematik*, pp. 281–288. Verlag Harri Deutsch, September 2000.

[124] A. Bjorck, *Numerical Methods for Least Squares Problems*. Society for Industrial & Applied Mathematics (SIAM), April 1996.

[125] N. Heldt, "Re-Engineering the Internet Gently," *I&C World*, vol. 12, December 2002.

[126] C. Hoogendoorn, K. Schrodi, M. Huber, C. Winkler, and J. Charzinski, "Towards Carrier-Grade Next Generation Networks," in *Proc. of International Conference on Communication Technology (ICCT)*, April 2003.

[127] S. Schnitter and M. Horneffer, "Traffic Matrices for MPLS Networks with LDP Traffic Statistics," in *Proc. of International Telecommunication Network Strategy and Planning Symposium (Networks)*, pp. 231–236, June 2004.

[128] S. Tomic, "Issues of Resource Management in Two-Layer GMPLS Networks with Virtual Network Services," in *Proc. of IEEE Global Telecommunications Conference (GLOBECOM)*, pp. 4035–4039, December 2004.

[129] M. Soleimanipour, W. Zhuang, and G. H. Freeman, "Optimal Resource Management in Multimedia WCDMA Systems," in *Proc. of IEEE Global Telecommunications Conference (GLOBECOM)*, pp. 1544–1547, November 2000.

[130] A. Hills and B. Friday, "Radio Resource Management in Wireless LANs," *IEEE Communications Magazine*, vol. 42, pp. 9–14, December 2004.

[131] A. Iera, A. Molinaro, and S. Marano, "Call Admission Control and Resource Management Issues for Real-Time VBR Traffic in ATM-Satellite Networks," *IEEE Journal on Selected Areas in Communications*, vol. 18, pp. 2393–2403, November 2000.

[132] ITU-T Recommendation Q.700, "Introduction to CCITT Signalling System No. 7," March 1993.

[133] A. Leon-Garcia and L. G. Mason, "Virtual Network Resource Management for Next-Generation Networks," *IEEE Communications Magazine*, vol. 41, pp. 102–109, July 2003.

[134] X. Xiao and L. M. Ni, "Internet QoS: A Big Picture," *IEEE Network Magazine*, vol. 13, pp. 8–18, March/April 1999.

[135] A. Conta, S. Deering, and M. Gupta, "RFC 4443: Internet Control Message Protocol (ICMPv6) for the Internet Protocol Version 6 (IPv6) Specification," March 2006.

[136] T. H. Henderson, E. Sahouria, S. McCanne, and R. H. Katz, "On Improving the Fairness of TCP Congestion Avoidance," in *Proc. of IEEE Global Telecommunications Conference (GLOBECOM)*, November 1998.

[137] M. Zhang, R. Wang, L. Peterson, and A. Krishnamurthy, "Probabilistic Packet Scheduling: Achieving Proportional Share Bandwidth Allocation for TCP Flows," in *Proc. of IEEE Conference on Computer Communications (INFOCOM)*, pp. 1650–1659, June 2002.

[138] B. Fortz and M. Thorup, "Internet Traffic Engineering by Optimizing OSPF Weights," in *Proc. of IEEE Conference on Computer Communications (INFOCOM)*, pp. 519–528, March 2000.

[139] S. Köhler, *Interior Gateway Routing Optimization and Quality of Service - Algorithms and Performance Study*. PhD thesis, University of Würzburg, November 2005.

[140] ANSI Document T1.105-2001, "Synchronous Optical Network - Basic Description Including Multiplex Structure, Rates, and Formats," 2001.

[141] ITU-T Recommendation G.707, "Network Node Interface for the Synchronous Digital Hierarchy (SDH)," December 2003.

[142] R. Ballart and Y.-C. Ching, "SONET: Now It's the Standard Optical Network," *IEEE Communications Magazine*, vol. 27, pp. 8–15, March 1989.

[143] R. Dutta and G. N. Rouskas, "Traffic Grooming in WDM Networks: Past and Future," *IEEE Network Magazine*, vol. 16, pp. 46–56, November 2002.

[144] O. J. Wasem, T.-H. Wu, and R. H. Cardwell, "Survivable SONET Networks-Design Methodology," *IEEE Journal on Selected Areas in Communications*, vol. 12, pp. 205–212, January 1994.

[145] T.-H. Wu and R. C. Lau, "A Class of Self-Healing Ring Architectures for SONET Network Applications," *IEEE Transactions on Communications*, vol. 40, pp. 1746–1756, November 1992.

[146] N. Ansari, G. Cheng, S. Israel, Y. Luo, J. Ma, and L. Zhu, "QoS Provision with Path Protection for Next Generation SONET," in *Proc. of IEEE International Conference on Communications (ICC)*, pp. 2152–2156, April 2002.

[147] D. Torrieri, "Algorithms for Finding an Optimal Set of Short Disjoint Paths in a Communication Network," *IEEE Transactions on Communications*, vol. 40, pp. 1698–1702, November 1992.

[148] B. Mukherjee, "WDM Optical Communication Networks: Progress and Challenges," *IEEE Journal on Selected Areas in Communications*, vol. 18, pp. 1810–1824, October 2000.

[149] B. Mukherjee, *Optical WDM Networks*. Springer, January 2006.

[150] R. Ramaswami and K. N. Sivarajan, "Routing and Wavelength Assignment in All-Optical Networks," *IEEE/ACM Transactions on Networking*, vol. 3, pp. 489–500, October 1995.

[151] J. M. Yates, M. P. Rumsewicz, and J. P. R. Lacey, "Wavelength Converters in Dynamically-Reconfigurable WDM Networks," *IEEE Communications Surveys & Tutorials*, vol. 2, pp. 2–15, April 1999.

[152] J. Zhang and B. Mukherjee, "A Review of Fault Management in WDM Mesh Networks: Basic Concepts and Research Challenges," *IEEE Network Magazine*, vol. 18, pp. 41–48, March/April 2004.

[153] P. P. White, "RSVP and Integrated Services in the Internet: A Tutorial," *IEEE Communications Magazine*, vol. 35, pp. 100–106, May 1997.

[154] F. Baker, C. Iturralde, F. Le Faucheur, and B. Davie, "RFC 3175: Aggregation of RSVP for IPv4 and IPv6 Reservations," September 2001.

[155] M. Günther and T. Braun, "Evaluation of Bandwidth Broker Signaling," in *Proc. of IEEE International Conference on Network Protocols (ICNP)*, pp. 145–152, November 1999.

[156] Z.-L. Zhang, Z. Duan, and Y. Hou, "On Scalable Design of Bandwidth Brokers," *IEICE Transaction on Communications*, vol. E84-B, pp. 2011–2025, August 2001.

[157] IETF Working Group on, "Multi-Protocol Label Switching (MPLS)." http://www.ietf.org/html.charters/mpls-charter.html.

[158] E. Osborne and A. Simha, *Traffic Engineering with MPLS*. Cisco Press, July 2002.

[159] T. Li, "MPLS and the Evolving Internet Architecture," *IEEE Communications Magazine*, vol. 37, pp. 38–41, December 1999.

[160] D. Allan *et al.*, "RFC 4378: A Framework for Multi-Protocol Label Switching (MPLS) Operations and Management (OAM)," February 2006.

[161] D. Cavendish, H. Ohta, and H. Rakotoranto, "Operation, Administration, and Maintenance in MPLS Networks," *IEEE Communications Magazine*, vol. 42, pp. 91–99, October 2004.

[162] T. D. Nadeau and M. J. Morrow, "MPLS Operations and Management," in *Proc. of IFIP/IEEE International Symposium on Integrated Network Management (IM)*, pp. 789–789, May 2005.

[163] P. Trimintzios *et al.*, "A Management and Control Architecture for Providing IP Differentiated Services in MPLS-Based Networks," *IEEE Communications Magazine*, vol. 39, pp. 80–88, May 2001.

[164] M. Kodialam and T. V. Lakshman, "Integrated Dynamic IP and Wavelength Routing in IP over WDM Networks," in *Proc. of IEEE Conference on Computer Communications (INFOCOM)*, pp. 358–366, April 2001.

[165] M. Brunner and C. Hullo, "GMPLS Fault Management and its Impact on Service Resilience Differentiation," in *Proc. of IFIP/IEEE International Symposium on Integrated Network Management (IM)*, pp. 665–678, March 2003.

[166] J. T. Park, "Resilience in GMPLS Path Management: Model and Mechanism," *IEEE Communications Magazine*, vol. 42, pp. 128–135, July 2004.

[167] P.-H. Ho and H. T. Mouftah, "Path Selection with Tunnel Allocation in the Optical internet Based on Generalized MPLS Architecture," in *Proc. of IEEE International Conference on Communications (ICC)*, pp. 2697–2701, April 2002.

[168] T. D. Nadeau and H. Rakotoranto, "GMPLS Operations and Management: Today's Challenges and Solutions for Tomorrow," *IEEE Communications Magazine*, vol. 43, July 2005.

[169] J. Y. Hui, "Resource Allocation for Broadband Networks," *IEEE Journal on Selected Areas in Communications*, vol. 6, pp. 1598–1608, December 1988.

[170] R. Guérin, H. Ahmadi, and M. Naghshineh, "Equivalent Capacity and Its Application to Bandwidth Allocation in High-Speed Networks," *IEEE Journal on Selected Areas in Communications*, vol. 9, pp. 968–981, September 1991.

[171] P. Siripongwutikorn, S. Banerjee, and D. Tipper, "A Survey of Adaptive Bandwidth Control Algorithms," *IEEE Communications Surveys & Tutorials*, vol. 5, pp. 14–26, June 2003.

[172] H. Tran and T. Ziegler, "On Adaptive Bandwidth Provisioning Schemes," in *Proc. of IEEE International Conference on Communications (ICC)*, June 2004.

[173] M. Pióro and D. Medhi, *Routing, Flow, and Capacity Design in Communication and Computer Networks*. Morgan Kaufmann, June 2004.

[174] A. Medina, N. Taft, K. Salamatian, S. Bhattacharyya, and C. Diot, "Traffic Matrix Estimation: Existing Techniques and New Directions," in *Proc. of ACM Special Interest Group on Data Communications (SIGCOMM)*, August 2002.

[175] D. Medhi, "Multi-Hour, Multi-Traffic Class Network Design for Virtual Path-Based Dynamically Reconfigurable Wide-Area ATM Networks," *IEEE/ACM Transactions on Networking*, vol. 3, pp. 809–818, December 1995.

[176] T. Bauschert, "Multi-Hour Design of Multi-Hop Virtual Path Based Wide-Area ATM Networks," in *Proc. of International Teletraffic Congress (ITC)*, June 1997.

[177] O. Heckmann, J. Schmitt, and R. Steinmetz, "Multi-Period Resource Allocation at System Edges," in *Proc. of International Conference on Telecommunication Systems, Modeling and Analysis (ICTSM)*, pp. 1–25, October 2002.

[178] B. G. Józsa, D. Orincsay, and L. Tamási, "Multi-Hour Design of Dynamically Reconfigurable MPLS networks," in *Proc. of IFIP-TC6 Networking Conference (NETWORKING)*, pp. 502–513, May 2004.

[179] D. Medhi and D. Tipper, "Some Approaches to Solving a Multi-hour Broadband Network Capacity Design Problem with Single-Path Routing," *IEEE/ACM Transactions on Networking*, vol. 13, pp. 269–291, April 2000.

[180] D. Zhemin, M. Hamdi, J. Y. B. Lee, and V. O. K. Li, "Integrated Routing and Grooming in GMPLS-Based Optical Networks," in *Proc. of IEEE International Conference on Communications (ICC)*, pp. 1584–1588, June 2004.

[181] A. Elwalid and D. Mitra, "Effective Bandwidth of General Markovian Traffic Sources and Admission Control of High Speed Networks," *IEEE/ACM Transactions on Networking*, vol. 1, pp. 329–343, June 1993.

[182] E. Gelenbe, X. Mang, and R. Önvural, "Bandwidth Allocation and Call Admission Control in High-Speed Networks," *IEEE Communications Magazine*, vol. 35, pp. 122–129, May 1997.

[183] R. Bolla, F. Davoli, and M. Marchese, "Bandwidth Allocation and Admission Control in ATM Networks with Service Separation," *IEEE Communications Magazine*, vol. 35, pp. 130–137, May 1997.

[184] G. de Veciana, G. Kesidis, and J. Walrand, "Resource Management in Wide-Area ATM Networks Using Effective Bandwidths," *IEEE Journal on Selected Areas in Communications*, vol. 13, pp. 1081–1090, August 1995.

[185] N. Anerousis and A. A. Lazar, "Virtual Path Control for ATM Networks with Call Level Quality of Service Guarantees," *IEEE/ACM Transactions on Networking*, vol. 6, pp. 222–236, April 1998.

[186] A. Arvidsson, "Real Time Management of Virtual Paths," in *Proc. of IEEE Global Telecommunications Conference (GLOBECOM)*, pp. 1399–1403, December 1994.

[187] K. Lu, G. Xiao, and I. Chlamtac, "Blocking Analysis of Dynamic Light-path Establishment in Wavelength-Routed Networks," in *Proc. of IEEE International Conference on Communications (ICC)*, pp. 2912–2916, April 2002.

[188] V. J. Friesen, J. J. Harms, and J. W. Wong, "Resource Management with Virtual Paths in ATM Networks," *IEEE Network Magazine*, vol. 10, pp. 10–20, September/October 1996.

[189] I. T. Okumus, J. Hwang, H. A. Mantar, and S. J. Chapin, "Inter-Domain LSP Setup Using Bandwidth Management Points," in *Proc. of IEEE Global Telecommunications Conference (GLOBECOM)*, pp. 7–11, November 2001.

[190] K. Shiomoto, S. Chaki, and N. Yamanaka, "A Simple Bandwidth Management Strategy Based on Measurements of Instantaneous Virtual Path Utilization in ATM Networks," *IEEE/ACM Transactions on Networking*, vol. 6, pp. 625–634, October 1998.

[191] P. Siripongwutikorn, S. Banerjee, and D. Tipper, "Adaptive Bandwidth Control for Efficient Aggregate QoS Provisioning," in *Proc. of IEEE Global Telecommunications Conference (GLOBECOM)*, pp. 2447–2451, November 2002.

[192] M. Menth, S. Gehrsitz, and J. Milbrandt, "Fair Assignment of Efficient Network Admission Control Budgets," in *Proc. of International Teletraffic Congress (ITC)*, pp. 1121–1130, September 2003.

[193] M. Menth, J. Milbrandt, and S. Kopf, "Capacity Assignment for NAC Budgets in Resilient Networks," in *Proc. of International Telecommunication Network Strategy and Planning Symposium (Networks)*, June 2004.

[194] A. Terzis, L. Zhang, and E. L. Hahne, "Reservations for Aggregate Traffic: Experiences from an RSVP Tunnels Implementation," in *Proc. of IEEE International Workshop on Quality of Service (IWQoS)*, May 1998.

[195] M. Menth, "A Scalable Protocol Architecture for End-to-End Signaling and Resource Reservation in IP Networks," in *Proc. of International Teletraffic Congress (ITC)*, pp. 211–222, December 2001.

[196] O. Heckmann, J. Schmitt, and R. Steinmetz, "Robust Bandwidth Allocation Strategies," in *Proc. of IEEE International Workshop on Quality of Service (IWQoS)*, June 2002.

[197] J. Milbrandt, M. Menth, and S. Kopf, "Adaptive Bandwidth Allocation: Concepts and Efficiency for Admission-Controlled Capacity Tunnels," in *Proc. of International Conference on Computing, Communications and Control Technologies (CCCT)*, July 2005.

[198] J. Milbrandt, M. Menth, and S. Kopf, "Adaptive Bandwidth Allocation: Impact of Traffic Demand Models for Wide Area Networks," in *Proc. of International Teletraffic Congress (ITC)*, August 2005.

[199] J. Milbrandt, K. Humm, and M. Menth, "Adaptive Bandwidth Allocation: Impact of Routing and Load Balancing on Tunnel Capacity Requirements," in *Proc. of Conference on Next Generation Internet Networks Traffic Engineering (NGI)*, April 2006.

[200] M. Menth, A. Reifert, and J. Milbrandt, "Self-Protecting Multipaths - A Simple and Resource-Efficient Protection Switching Mechanism for MPLS Networks," in *Proc. of IFIP-TC6 Networking Conference (NETWORKING)*, May 2004.

[201] D. Eppstein, "Finding the k Shortest Paths," in *Proc. of IEEE Symposium on Foundations of Computer Science (FOCS)*, pp. 154–165, November 1994.

[202] J. W. Suurballe, "Disjoint paths in a network," *Networks Magazine*, vol. 4, pp. 125–145, 1974.

[203] J. Milbrandt, R. Martin, M. Menth, and F. Höhn, "Risk Assessment of End-to-End Disconnection in IP Networks due to Network Failures," in *Proc. of IEEE International Workshop on IP Operations and Management (IPOM)*, October 2006.

[204] M. Menth, J. Milbrandt, and F. Lehrieder, "Algorithms for Fast Resilience Analysis in IP Networks," in *Proc. of IEEE International Workshop on IP Operations and Management (IPOM)*, October 2006.

[205] J. Milbrandt, M. Menth, and F. Lehrieder, "A Priori Detection of Link Overload due to Network Failures." Under submission.

Bibliography